This journal belongs to

_____

A Garden of Hope

DEVOTIONAL JOURNAL

BELLE CITY GIFTS

Belle City Gifts
Racine, Wisconsin, USA

Belle City Gifts is an imprint of BroadStreet Publishing Group LLC.
Broadstreetpublishing.com

A Garden of Hope

© 2015 by Sandy Lynam Clough

ISBN 978-1-4245-5001-2 (hard cover)
ISBN 978-1-4245-5043-2 (e-book)

Design by Chris Garborg | www.garborgdesign.com
Artwork by Sandy Lynam Clough | www.sandyclough.com
Editorial services by Michelle Winger | www.literallyprecise.com

Printed in China.

15 16 17 18 19 20 21 | 7 6 5 4 3 2 1

Introduction

The garden of life is not as perfect as we would like it to be. Yet within it, God has painted pictures of faith, hope, love, and, yes, even correction in the places it's needed. The devotions in this book illustrate lessons that cannot be painted with a paintbrush; they are painted instead with words.

Read the words written here and as you reflect on them, realize that God is everything you need. Life that seems so imperfect is full of beauty, for it has been perfectly designed as an invitation for you to grow closer to God.

Hope in Your Character and Love for Me

A beautiful English garden overflowing with cascades of my favorite flowers, alive with the fluttering and floating of birds and butterflies, and awash with fragrance—I would have chosen that for a picture of the life I always hoped to have. A garden of perfection with perfect weather, abundance, and season after season filled with only delights. A garden of comfort. A garden of joy. A painting I could have walked into and lived my dreams of a perfect life.

Lord, my life is not my creation. It is yours, and you watch over it carefully. Although there has been much beauty and more joy, there have also been storms and droughts, broken branches and unsprouted seeds, tenacious weeds and even pests in the garden of my life. Yet all of it, sunshine and rain, draws me to know you. Each brand new problem, each new blow in my life seems at first unsolvable, draining all the hope out of the room. But every new storm causes me to run to you because instinctively I know that you are the only one who can help—even though I can't imagine what the help will look like.

As I read your Word searching, searching for whatever hope you will give me, I see you…more of you. The beauty of your character, your constant love for me, your faithfulness, your wisdom. You are hope. You are everything that I need. I can trust you. My wounds will heal. The beauty will come back. Joy will inhabit it.

As I go forward with more confidence in you, my compassion grows for all those around me with both fresh wounds and stiff challenges. I find myself carrying your heart in my own—wanting to share it with those who hurt—pouring out hope from a garden hose attached to your endless supply. This is the kind of hope we only find in desperation.

"THIS IS THE WAY TO HAVE ETERNAL LIFE—BY KNOWING YOU, THE ONLY TRUE GOD, AND JESUS CHRIST, THE ONE YOU SENT TO EARTH!" (JOHN 17:3, TLB)

Your life that may seem imperfect is full of beauty.
How do you see your life as an invitation for you to know God more deeply?

_____

_____

_____

_____

_____

_____

_____

_____

_____

_____

_____

_____

_____

_____

_____

_____

_____

_____

Healing from Hurt

I am tempted to plant my hurts in clay pots where they would like to be displayed for all to see. Then, I could have sympathy and my friends would say, "Bless her heart." But I don't want my life to be defined by my hurts. I don't want them to be the first thing people see when they look at me. I want to be a voice for your healings and help, Lord. So, instead I will plant those hurts in my hope garden and water them with your Word. In this process, as your Word shows me your heart, the ugly seeds of hurt sprout into flowers of trust in you. As they mature, those flowers bear seeds of hope! You completely transform what was started as hurtful into something good for me.

Now, I can carry my hurts, not as baggage, but as a first aid kit. I can use the stories to connect the wounded people I meet to your tender care and assure them of your faithfulness. Because of you, hurts that could have darkened days of my life are now stored, not in resentfulness, but in a seed bank of hope. In this kind of garden, the same seed can be planted over and over again.

Please make me a careful gardener who has a doctor's motto: First, do no damage. Help me to pay close attention to those around me and be very selective of the help I offer—realizing that all my seeds don't fit in their garden. I especially want to be careful not to bruise them with careless chatter. Help me remember that sometimes just an understanding silence is a welcome cushion for a hurting heart. I ask you for opportunities to connect other wounded hearts to my stories of your watchful care and your transforming love.

WHAT A WONDERFUL GOD WE HAVE—HE IS THE FATHER OF OUR LORD JESUS CHRIST, THE SOURCE OF EVERY MERCY, AND THE ONE WHO SO WONDERFULLY COMFORTS AND STRENGTHENS US IN OUR HARDSHIPS AND TRIALS. AND WHY DOES HE DO THIS? SO THAT WHEN OTHERS ARE TROUBLED, NEEDING OUR SYMPATHY AND ENCOURAGEMENT, WE CAN PASS ON TO THEM THIS SAME HELP AND COMFORT GOD HAS GIVEN US (2 CORINTHIANS 1:3, TLB).

Are there people in your life who just need you to listen?
How can you best love and care for them?

_____

_____

_____

_____

_____

_____

_____

_____

_____

_____

_____

_____

_____

_____

_____

Purity

Feeding the hummingbirds keeps them close to our garden. They are a wonder to watch. They stretch my mind as I try to imagine how you designed them, Lord, and how you conceived of their entertaining ways. As I count out one-two-three-four measures of water to add to the sugar for them, I wonder, *Should I be using bottled spring water instead of tap water?* After all, these exquisitely beautiful yet incredibly petite birds have tiny metabolisms. Can they tolerate the impurities that might be lurking in tap water?

It was a noble thought—pure, bottled water for the hummingbirds. But the real question bubbled up in my heart. How careful am I about the purity of things I allow in my mind, my heart, and my spirit? If it's garbage in-garbage out for a computer, it must be the same for me. Can I really let entertainment pour immorality and violence into my eyes and ears and not damage my soul? Psalm 101:3 contains a commitment to put no evil thing before my eyes.

Lord, I'm asking you to sensitize me to recognize the pollution of the toxic sounds and images I am bombarded with. As they become more and more common, I don't want to be numbed to their effect. You have washed my heart and mind. You made me a brand new creature when you came into my life. I want to stay squeaky clean and filter out anything that isn't pleasing to you, keeping my heart as a dwelling place that you are comfortable in.

DON'T COPY THE BEHAVIOR AND CUSTOMS OF THIS WORLD, BUT LET GOD TRANSFORM YOU INTO A NEW PERSON BY CHANGING THE WAY YOU THINK. THEN YOU WILL LEARN TO KNOW GOD'S WILL FOR YOU, WHICH IS GOOD AND PLEASING AND PERFECT (ROMANS 12:2, NLT).

Do you find yourself becoming numb to the toxic fumes of the world?
Thank the Lord for his cleansing of your heart and mind.

A Larger World

As a child, I don't think I considered what was going on in my mother's world, in her plans, her thoughts, her dreams. It seemed to me that her world revolved around me—just as my own did. She and my father did so much to ensure I had every advantage they could provide, so I might reach my potential. Yet I never asked what their idea of "potential" was or questioned her specifically to tell me about her heart or her purposes. I missed so much by not realizing that my nurturing revolved around my mother and father and the purposes in their hearts.

I suppose it is the way of children to care only about their small world. Lord, although I am your child, I don't want to have a childish heart that sees me as the center of your world. It is true that you have given me far more than I fully grasp. Your Father's heart has created me, loved me, redeemed me, and has planned the days of my life and even my eternity.
I don't have words to describe the wonder of you adopting me as your very own child. You are involved in every aspect of my life.

It is my life that must revolve around you. Let me never make the mistake of thinking this is all about me. You are master, king of kings, the everlasting Lord. It is my place to completely put myself in your hands and to fit into your world as you please.

I urge you, brothers and sisters, in view of God's mercy, to offer your bodies as a living sacrifice, holy and pleasing to God—this is your true and proper worship (Romans 12:1, niv).

Is the ultimate potential for your life to know and love God?
How can you show him this?

Helpless

Lord, I confess that sometimes there are days when everything around me seems hopeless and I feel a little hopeless myself. But hopeless really isn't the right word for it because I'm not without hope. What I really am is *helpless*. I am helpless to determine my own destiny, to guarantee my security, to control everything spinning around me. Helpless, however, is a really good place to be. Being helpless doesn't mean that I'm without help. It's a place where I can rest and be totally dependent on you, my Heavenly Father. Because you are not only my help, you're a *present* help—here, now, always.

At a time when I knew that if you didn't help me there would be no help for me, you assured me that you are both willing and able to help me in so many ways. In Hebrews 13:5, you promise not to leave me helpless or to let go of me. You hear me when I call for help. You deliver me from my fears. You are a refuge for me and a stronghold in trouble. You are a hiding place for me and I have your steadfast love that prevails over everything else. You are my rock and my salvation. Because your words and promises are pure words, I can lean on you. Even though in my own strength I may feel helpless, because my trust is in you I have every kind of help I will ever need.

Because you are my helper,
I sing for joy in the shadow of your wings (Psalm 63:7, nlt).

How would you describe the difference between being *hopeless* and being *helpless*?
Do you see the strength that is available to you when you are *helpless*?

Rain in the Garden

A shower is gently washing everything in the garden. The birdbath is slowly filling up. How the birds will love the refreshment of it as they splash around and sip the water! The daisy doesn't droop to hide its face from the drops, but instead honestly holds up its face. It is not broken, but is washed by the rain and left with a sprinkling of sparkling raindrops.

Yet my own heart droops under the realization that my recent behavior has been so unlike you, Lord. I'd like to hide it rather than own it, but it is there like a cloud blocking our fellowship. I'm tempted to forge on and try to ignore it, but we both know there must be a time when I make things right with you. Even if I excuse myself for what I've done, ultimately I will have to come right back to this place and deal with this with you.

I must confess it now—agreeing with you where I was wrong—and as I tell you what you already know, I am being gently washed. My heart softens as I agree with yours, and I am willing to apologize to those I offended and tell them what they already know—that I was wrong.

Now, like the daisy, I can lift my own head honestly toward your light. The barrier between us has vanished and life has its sparkle again.

IF WE SAY THAT WE HAVE NO SIN, WE DECEIVE OURSELVES, AND THE TRUTH IS NOT IN US. IF WE CONFESS OUR SINS, HE IS FAITHFUL AND JUST TO FORGIVE US OUR SINS AND TO CLEANSE US FROM ALL UNRIGHTEOUSNESS (1 JOHN 1:8-9, NKJV).

Is something hindering you from lifting your face toward the light of the Lord? Confess it to God and allow his forgiveness to make you shine again!

After the Storm

The storm has blown over, but my garden is a mess. It will take some work and some time to rake up the damage and debris. After the broken branches are pruned and removed, it will actually look neater—and cleaner than it did before the storm. More light will get in. The wilted and withered plants will have to be pulled up, but that will make room for more growth. There has been loss, but the life of the garden is intact. It will recover with enough time and care.

Just as a garden that has been buffeted by a storm, it's not enough for my personal storm to stop. Lord, I need your restoration. As I concentrate on your Word and talk with you, reveal to me if there are any broken parts of my life that need to be pruned and let go of. I'm willing to remove any wrong behavior, careless speech, bad memories—anything that I might have added to the storm. As far as I know, this storm has nothing of my making. It has come from circumstances I cannot predict or control.

My prayer is that you will restore me in the places where I cannot heal myself. Tie bandages of forgiveness and forgetfulness around my hurts just as I would bandage a broken branch or gently replace an uprooted flower. I trust you to take advantage of this for me in ways I can't see right now. Thank you for all the tender care you give me.

I AM PERSUADED THAT NEITHER DEATH NOR LIFE, NOR ANGELS NOR PRINCIPALITIES NOR POWERS, NOR THINGS PRESENT NOR THINGS TO COME, NOR HEIGHT NOR DEPTH, NOR ANY OTHER CREATED THING, SHALL BE ABLE TO SEPARATE US FROM THE LOVE OF GOD WHICH IS IN CHRIST JESUS OUR LORD (ROMANS 8:38-39, NKJV).

In what areas do you need to let the light of hope make your future look more promising? Do you trust God to restore you?

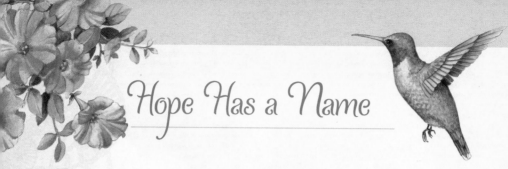

Hope Has a Name

There are plants that live in my garden that I cannot identify. They are anonymous. I don't know what they are. The problem is if I don't know a plant's name, I don't know what it needs from me. I'm clueless as to how to reference it, how to care for it, or what to expect from it. Will this be its only appearance, or will it be back next year? What if it isn't a flower after all, but actually a weed that I shouldn't encourage?

There are things that sprout up in my life, as well, that I don't know how to name. Has an opportunity come to me or a distraction? Am I investing my time in a blessing or a regret? Is tomorrow joy, or is tomorrow trouble? In this uncertain world, it's hard to identify everything and give it a definitive name.

Thankfully, I have no confusion about hope because the hope that lives in me is not anonymous. Hope has a name, and it is Jesus, the name above all names. I know what to expect from you, Lord Jesus. I can expect you to be everything that you are in my life. I know what you need from me is to surrender to your will and your purposes. Lord, I gladly give you the ownership of the garden of my heart, knowing that I can completely trust you with the results. You are everything I need.

ALL HONOR TO GOD, THE GOD AND FATHER OF OUR LORD JESUS CHRIST; FOR IT IS HIS BOUNDLESS MERCY THAT HAS GIVEN US THE PRIVILEGE OF BEING BORN AGAIN SO THAT WE ARE NOW MEMBERS OF GOD'S OWN FAMILY. NOW WE LIVE IN THE HOPE OF ETERNAL LIFE BECAUSE CHRIST ROSE AGAIN FROM THE DEAD (1 PETER 1:3, TLB).

How can you apply the definitive hope you have in Jesus
to the anonymous circumstances of life?

Safe in the Nest

Every evening, a little bird flutters up under the eaves to our porch, fluffs his feathers, and nestles in for the night. Whether the night is stormy or starry, he rests securely. I can rest as securely as he does, for there is no storm that can overwhelm your care for me, Lord. Your loving-kindness prevails over me. It's true that I don't know where every storm is, or when it might come my way, but you know where *I* am.

I'm not sure if it matters to the bird whether we're here or not. He may only want the shelter our porch affords. I long for more than comfort and shelter from storms, though. My heart wants to be in your presence, Lord, like the sparrow in Psalm 84. The psalmist had the same yearning; he wanted to be in your courts where he could sing to you for joy. He said that the sparrow found a house there and the swallow a nest. And that those who dwell in your house and in your presence are blessed to sing your praises all the day long!

I come into your presence with singing, Lord—with songs of thanksgiving for your goodness and songs of praise. There are no words or songs that are adequate praise for you. Even so, your Word teaches me how to tune my heart to bless you. I'm encouraged to sing joyfully, to sing of your righteousness, your strength, your love, your justice, the glory of your name! It is my joy to sing to you with a heart of love and gratitude.

I will exalt you, my God and King,
and praise your name forever and ever.
I will praise you every day;
yes, I will praise you forever.
Great is the Lord! He is most worthy of praise!
No one can measure his greatness (Psalm 145:1-3, nlt).

Can you let yourself rest securely in God's care for you no matter what the day brings? Tell God how grateful you are for his protection.

All Things for Good

Romans 8:28 tells me that you cause all things to work together for good to those who love you, Lord, to those who are called according to your purpose. How often I've heard well-meaning people use this verse to say that you make bad things into good things. That is hard for people suffering devastating loss to hear! How could a hurting person comprehend a tragic loss as being a good thing?

The promise I hear in this verse is not that "bad becomes good," but rather that you will work things together for *good to me*—and everyone who is yours—even when I suffer loss. There is such real comfort in that promise! You are bringing good to me no matter what happens.

It is tempting to exhaust myself trying to figure what that good might be and when it might happen. Trying to figure it out is a good way to disappoint myself, too, when the "good" I imagine hasn't happened. I admit that I am impatient to see the good you are working for me. I am more than curious to know how you will take advantage of my losses! But what I have learned is that when your good for me becomes apparent, it will be more wonderful than anything I could have imagined!

My hope is anchored in the knowledge that you will take whatever happens to me and work it into your purposes for me. Nothing is wasted in this process. You are the author of my life and I trust you with my story!

We know that God causes all things to work together for good to those who love God, to those who are called according to His purpose (Romans 8:28, nasb).

What good things have you seen God work in your life when you were struggling?

_____

_____

_____

_____

_____

_____

_____

_____

_____

_____

_____

_____

_____

_____

_____

_____

_____

_____

_____

_____

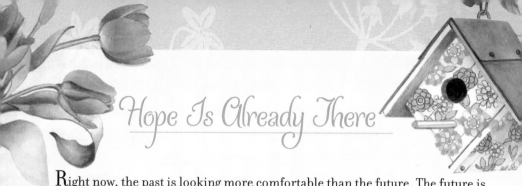

Hope Is Already There

Right now, the past is looking more comfortable than the future. The future is begging for hope! I can function in the present and in what I know about it. I know I can because I'm doing it. The past doesn't need any hope. The hope the past needed when it was the future has been replaced with a solid record of your faithfulness, Lord. But the future is another thing. It must have hope!

I'm watching an autumn leaf valiantly try to hang on to a branch in the chilling wind, and the nearly bare branches looked to be stripped of life and hope. But wait—even though the last leaf has not fallen, I can see that you are already putting the buds of the spring leaves on the branch. It will be a while until spring, but the hope of spring is already here!

Lord, you are not only the creator of that tree and the promise of springtime and harvest, you are the Good Shepherd. My shepherd. You go ahead of me whether my life is passing through a shadowy valley or a sunlit meadow. You will care for me and comfort me. If a stormy patch batters me, you will restore me and make me a good example of your grace and faithfulness. Right now, the tomorrows around the bend don't look that promising. There are serious challenges to be acknowledged. Even so, I can face the future with confidence since you are already there. Because you are there, hope is already there too.

"I KNOW THE PLANS I HAVE FOR YOU," DECLARES THE LORD, "PLANS TO PROSPER YOU AND NOT TO HARM YOU, PLANS TO GIVE YOU HOPE AND A FUTURE" (JEREMIAH 29:11, NIV).

Consider your past and God's faithfulness to you.
How does his faithfulness bring hope to your future?

Sifting the Seeds

Our birdseed is actually a blend of different seeds mingled and mixed together to entice a variety of birds. Instinctively, each kind of bird will pick through the seeds to find which seeds are right for it and then ruthlessly toss aside any other that is in its way—creating a buffet for the doves, chipmunks, and squirrels on the ground. Lord, it is a wonder to me how you have created each bird to know which food is right for them and have given them an appetite for it.

There is quite a mixture of teachings swirling around me. Some of it sounds so good, but at its essence seems to be bad seed—suggesting I try to manipulate you with your own words to do *my* will and *my* pleasure. But focusing on me brings me right back to living in my own selfishness, which is where I started before I began my life as a Christian. Your Spirit in me is helping me discern and sift through this culture of "me." It draws a lot of crowds and is so popular, but if I listen closely, it is suggesting that you serve *me* instead of me serving *you*. That I am the pearl of great price instead of you.

That teaching cannot be food for me. Your Word says that I am to love you with all my heart, mind, soul, and spirit. My greatest hope is choosing your ways and purposes above my own. That is where I will find blessing.

DON'T LET ANYONE CAPTURE YOU WITH EMPTY PHILOSOPHIES AND HIGH-SOUNDING NONSENSE THAT COME FROM HUMAN THINKING AND FROM THE SPIRITUAL POWERS OF THIS WORLD, RATHER THAN FROM CHRIST (COLOSSIANS 2:8, NLT).

How can you weigh up the validity of different teachings in your life?
How can you discern what is truth?

Annual or Perennial

One of the first things I learned about gardening was the basic knowledge that most plants are either annuals that bloom their hearts out all season and then don't come back, or perennials that bloom for a shorter time but come back faithfully year after year. The annuals make up for their short run by being colorful and showy—so much so that I'm willing to buy them over and over every spring. The perennials, on the other hand, are so faithful and dependable that the garden really needs them, even though their "time to shine" is shorter.

Am I like an annual? Or a perennial? I've seen some annual Christians who get excited and create a buzz about the important things they are doing. But then, they seem to fade away. Lord, I'm more drawn to the perennials who serve you steadily year after year. They seem to be more grounded and rooted in you even though their walk isn't always "showy." They bloom according to your schedule and then are content to connect to you in quieter times on a deeper and deeper level as you develop and grow them. In season, and out of season, they are constant and dependable. I want to be the perennial Christian who is steady and develops like a plant strong enough to drop good seeds, year after year, that sprout into other perennials that are committed to you for the long run.

JUST AS YOU ACCEPTED CHRIST JESUS AS YOUR LORD, YOU MUST CONTINUE TO FOLLOW HIM. LET YOUR ROOTS GROW DOWN INTO HIM, AND LET YOUR LIVES BE BUILT ON HIM. THEN YOUR FAITH WILL GROW STRONG IN THE TRUTH YOU WERE TAUGHT, AND YOU WILL OVERFLOW WITH THANKFULNESS (COLOSSIANS 2:6-7, NLT).

Ask yourself truthfully if you are more like an annual or perennial.
How can you maintain your commitment to God in each season of life?

_____

_____

_____

_____

_____

_____

_____

_____

_____

_____

_____

_____

_____

_____

_____

_____

_____

_____

How Can I Trust You?

Lord, how can I trust you when everything keeps getting worse? That heart cry is sometimes spoken and so often unspoken. It is a hanging question—how? How can I trust? In my own heart it found a voice when there was a threat to my vision. What were you thinking? What were you planning? How could I figure it all out?

I had to know one thing. I had to know that you are good. When I turned to your Word to confirm your goodness to my heart, I found your heart and your character. In the book of Psalms, I found the answer to all my questions. Do you hear me when I pray? You hear me when I call. (See Psalm 4:3.) You have plans for me that you will accomplish. (See Psalm 138:8.) My heart found the strength of confidence in your very character. It was then that fear was replaced with hope that wasn't based on my circumstances. My discouragement was replaced with praise. My how-to-trust questions were answered by a new awareness of your personal love for me.

It seems a little upside down but when I concentrate on you, I find the assurance that your thoughts are on me and you have everything about me under control. You completely end the nightmare I experience from circumstances without changing the circumstances. Then you bless me and let me see your goodness. I don't look at my circumstances for hope, I know that my hope and confidence are in your character and that is how I can trust you.

DO NOT THROW AWAY YOUR CONFIDENCE, WHICH HAS A GREAT REWARD (HEBREWS 10:35, NASB).

Is your trust placed confidently in the Lord? What do you feel when you hear that his thoughts are on you and that he has everything under control?

_____

_____

_____

_____

_____

_____

_____

_____

_____

_____

_____

_____

_____

_____

_____

_____

_____

_____

_____

_____

Snake in the Garden

I was startled to see a snake cozied up in the broken brick wall around my garden, sunning his scaly head. Before he could be dispatched, he wiggled down out of sight in the honeycombed wall, taking the carefree joy of my garden with him. Now, instead of walking right into my garden to check for new blooms, my first concern became to watch my step, and to make sure he wasn't inspecting a bird's nest in the top of the arbor or coiled underneath my roses.

The next time I saw him venturing forth from his hiding place, he *was* dispatched (by the men in the family) to the far, far reaches of our woods—far enough for me to believe he couldn't find his way back. I had my garden back! Why, in the midst of acres of woods teeming with hapless mice, rocks for sunning, and a creek for water sports, was he here? Perhaps it was the little unsuspecting chipmunks scampering in my garden that made him want to settle in. For him, it was an opportunity.

Lord, help me to remember there is always a serpent, my enemy, who wishes to take up residence in my life, replacing your agenda for me with his own. Let me walk carefully, recognizing the choices that could give him an opportunity. Remind me of your Word when I need to identify him immediately. Alert me to the sin and broken places in my life that might provide him a place to settle in, that I might repent and repair them, denying him any comfort zone.

GIVE YOURSELVES HUMBLY TO GOD. RESIST THE DEVIL AND HE WILL FLEE FROM YOU (JAMES 4:7, TLB).

Are you constantly on the lookout for the enemy?
What can you do to minimize his opportunity to take up residence in your life?

_____

_____

_____

_____

_____

_____

_____

_____

_____

_____

_____

_____

_____

_____

_____

_____

_____

_____

_____

_____

Beauty

My southern mother had a word for my childhood behavior if I pitched a fit, whined, or sulked: "Don't act *ugly!*" I'm not sure I could have verbally defined what ugly was, but I knew what it was. I knew which behavior could get the look from my mother. It was the opposite of "pretty is as pretty does."

As an adult, I finally made the connection between acting ugly as a child and sin. There is nothing casual or neutral about sin. Sin is ugly. And it looks terribly unflattering on me. Even the word *sin* sounds ugly. Come to think of it, when I am angry, or resentful, or disagreeable, I never want to look in a mirror. Or worse, want a photo taken. I think that instinctively I know that something unattractive has taken over my face—something that is unbecoming.

I refuse to tolerate habits of sin and let them write their unhappiness on my face over time. Instead, Lord, I want your character to reign in me displaying its own beauty. The fruit of your Spirit offers me much to light up my countenance: love, joy, peace, longsuffering, kindness, goodness, faithfulness, meekness, and self-control. No cosmetic can compete with the beauty of that. Sooner or later, what is in my heart will be written on my face. If it is a deep knowledge of you, it will be beautiful.

DON'T BE CONCERNED ABOUT THE OUTWARD BEAUTY THAT DEPENDS ON JEWELRY, OR BEAUTIFUL CLOTHES, OR HAIR ARRANGEMENT. BE BEAUTIFUL INSIDE, IN YOUR HEARTS, WITH THE LASTING CHARM OF A GENTLE AND QUIET SPIRIT THAT IS SO PRECIOUS TO GOD (1 PETER 3:3-4, TLB).

Can you see true and lasting beauty within yourself?
How do you see God's character reigning in your life?

Joy

Watchman Nee had been imprisoned for his faith for 20 years when he wrote "I maintain my joy." The day he died he wrote, "I still remain joyful at heart." I think that seems hard to understand because it's so easy to get *happy* mixed up with *joy*. *Happy* is the wonderful feeling that makes laughter and giggles bubble up and causes a smile that can't be stifled. We all want happy! But happy in a prison? I can imagine episodes of happiness, but not sustained happiness. Happiness is an elusive thing that comes and goes. It's just not sustainable because it is dependent on my circumstances, which I cannot control.

Joy is different. I'm learning that it's *not* dependent on my circumstances. There is a secret to joy and I believe this is it: if I take "I maintain my joy" and switch out one word, it makes all the difference: "I maintain my *relationship*." Joy can be constant as my relationship with you is constant. Joy isn't just something you have, Lord. It is part of who you are, and it flows from you to me!

Joy as a feeling is difficult to describe. It's peace, yet more than contentment. It's hope, yet it's more than optimism. It's more resonant than happiness and much more than the knowledge that we do win in the end. Joy is you in my heart.

Joy is something you really want us to have and you ask the Father to give it to us!

I SAY THESE THINGS WHILE I AM STILL IN THE WORLD, SO THAT MY JOY MAY BE MADE FULL *AND* COMPLETE *AND* PERFECT IN THEM [THAT THEY MAY EXPERIENCE MY DELIGHT FULFILLED IN THEM, THAT MY ENJOYMENT MAY BE PERFECTED IN THEIR OWN SOULS, THAT THEY MAY HAVE MY GLADNESS WITHIN THEM, FILLING THEIR HEARTS] (JOHN 17:13, AMP).

How do you feel when you experience the joy that comes from the Lord?
Ask the Father today for more joy than you can contain!

_____

_____

_____

_____

_____

_____

_____

_____

_____

_____

_____

_____

_____

_____

_____

_____

_____

_____

_____

Sound of the Garden

Some add the cheerfulness of chimes, bells, and whirligigs to their gardens to catch the breeze. That way they can *hear* the wind with whirrs, clinks, or chimes. Without these musical sounds, they might never be aware of the breeze softly blowing across the garden, slightly ruffling the leaves.

Can I hear the wind or breeze of your Holy Spirit moving in my life? Or am I making so much noise of my own—like a clanging bell or a clinking cymbal—that I am missing you? Missing the still, small voice.

Being quiet and listening is hard—really hard. My mind races about. There's a call I need to make, or something to get from the store. Walking outside with only the birds singing, the leaves fluttering, and the squirrels crunching leaves as they scurry, just that music and nothing more, helps me to be quiet and listen. I listen to my own heart and remember what I want to praise you for. I hear your prompting to pray for someone's need. I start to count everything I am thankful for.

There is a wonderful song about walking in a garden and talking with you and the joy it brings. A garden seems like a perfect place to spend the time I need with you. Yet, there doesn't even have to be a garden, just a heart that wants to turn down the volume of the world and take the time to talk to you and to listen. And I do.

My voice You shall hear in the morning, O Lord;
In the morning I will direct it to You,
And I will look up (Psalm 5:3, nkjv).

Are you aware of God's presence in your life?
What can you do to truly hear his voice among the noise of life?

_____

_____

_____

_____

_____

_____

_____

_____

_____

_____

_____

_____

_____

_____

_____

_____

Broken Hearts

Not long ago, I noticed a bag they were giving out at the hospital that said "We mend broken hearts." I thought, *Really? Can they really do that? Surely not for everyone.* But *you* can, Lord. And only you can.

I can protect my most fragile possessions by putting them behind glass or stashing them in a drawer. My heart, though, is a different matter. There is no failsafe place to hide it. No place to stuff it away where it can't be chipped, cracked, or broken. And it has been.

I may not look chipped or cracked, but you see these invisible scars. You saw the wounds when they happened. It was you who bound them up. It is you who can prevent the infection of bitterness from festering in the fresh hurt. It is you who heals every wound until the remembered scar has no pain and the memory of it can no longer make me wince.

It is you who enables me to thank you for each one, because each one helped me know you better. When I have shared a story of coming from pain to peace with a hurting soul, I've found that everyone is comfortable with someone who is chipped and dinged. I'm not volunteering for more heart problems, Lord, but I offer the ones that I've had to you to help heal other hearts.

THE LORD IS CLOSE TO THOSE WHOSE HEARTS ARE BREAKING; HE RESCUES THOSE WHO ARE HUMBLY SORRY FOR THEIR SINS (PSALM 34:18, TLB).

Are you going through a season of suffering?
Ask the Lord to be near to you in your time of need.

Keeping the Fragrance

In the spring, the rose bushes in our garden cloak themselves in hundreds of blooms that cascade over the brick wall. The fragrance drifts out to meet me if I just walk by, beckoning me to come closer and breathe in the fragrance of a single rose. The one I always choose is the one richest in perfume—Madam Isaac Pereire—named for the wife of a French banker. This wonderful fragrance has scented gardens since 1881 never losing its essence. It is an antique rose, propagated by cuttings as friends and families shared its beauty.

Experienced gardeners can combine certain qualities of two different roses and create new, different hybrids with grafting or cross pollination. Although they are beautiful to look at, many hybrid roses have lost the fragrance of the original roses in the process.

Father, your Word says that I, your child, am the sweet fragrance of Christ in the world around me. I confess, though, that I can be distracted by other Christians around me who minister, teach, and share. They seem so good at it. Peppering their messages with humor and great stories, their presentation is impressive. They have style. What I can offer seems to be less.

The difference between antique and hybrid roses is helping me see that if I focus on trying to re-configure your message or try to impress with my own clever presentation, I can engineer your fragrance right out of what I'm doing! I don't want my life to be a hybrid of you and me that is actually nothing more than my version of you. The fragrance that is purely you, simply expressed in my personality, is the one that attracts others to the vital life you offer them.

NOW THANKS BE TO GOD WHO ALWAYS LEADS US IN TRIUMPH IN CHRIST, AND THROUGH US DIFFUSES THE FRAGRANCE OF HIS KNOWLEDGE IN EVERY PLACE (2 CORINTHIANS 2:14, NKJV).

How do you maintain the sweet fragrance of Christ in the world around you?

Standing and Praying

Lord, there such a constant need for prayer that I confess I find myself longing for a break—a time when trouble is out of season. A time when I could coast a little or drift along with no emergency room issues, no strongholds resisting your will. A time when I could love and thank you without urgently calling on your help and intervention.

I'm beginning to understand that focused prayer never goes out of season. It shouldn't go out of season. It must not go out of season. You have placed me where I am because you want me to stand in my place of prayer and to be your person here.

In John 15, you tell us how to abide in you. Just as the branches of my rose bushes receive their life from the plant's trunk, I receive my life flow and nourishment through my connection to you, the true vine. You created plants to not only have life and bear fruit but to also remove carbon dioxide from the air and replace it with life-giving oxygen. I'm learning that in much the same way, my prayers can gather the noxious air of the situations around me and bring them to you to be transformed.

Lord, I choose to take my responsibility and stand in the place where you have me. Even if I find myself surrounded by poison in the spiritual atmosphere, I will gather up every toxic thing that threatens my family and opposes you, and I will bring them to you in prayer. I trust you to transform them from spiritual death to spiritual life.

IF YOU REMAIN IN ME AND MY WORDS REMAIN IN YOU, YOU MAY ASK FOR ANYTHING YOU WANT, AND IT WILL BE GRANTED! (JOHN 15:7, NLT)

What toxic things are threatening your spiritual growth right now? Stand in the place of prayer and be transformed by the nourishment of your connection to the true vine.

_____

_____

_____

_____

_____

_____

_____

_____

_____

_____

_____

_____

_____

_____

_____

_____

_____

_____

Busyness

Around and around they go—buzzing and humming and fluttering! The birds and bugs in my garden are always on the go! But I can't really blame them. It's what they have to do to survive. Whether it's sipping nectar or pecking at seeds, it's what they do for a living.

What is it, though, that makes me (and everyone around me) so very, very busy? We are all so frantically busy that even *hobbies* have gone out of style! Yes, jobs, meals, ministry, and parenting are all necessary to life, but what about the rest? I've heard it said that if Satan can't make me bad, he'll make me busy. I'm sure he knows that busyness is the best way to get me to miss my time with you every day and neglect your priorities.

Will you help me evaluate the way I am spending my time from your perspective? Please speak to my heart as I sift each thing in my routine by asking these questions:

Does this need to be done to maintain life?
Is this your idea, my idea, or someone else's idea?
Will it matter when I stand before you?
Is it my calling?
Is it my duty?
Does it count for joy?
Is there something else I'm *not* doing that you want me to do?

Your Word says that you have already planned and written out my days. Show me how not to just spend them, but to use them the way you planned.

Teach us to number our days and recognize how few they are; help us to spend them as we should (Psalm 90:12, TLB).

Evaluate the way you spend your time by asking yourself the same questions.

_____
_____
_____
_____
_____
_____
_____
_____
_____
_____
_____
_____
_____
_____
_____
_____
_____
_____
_____

Leaning

My dahlias and hollyhocks are brave and optimistic as they stretch their stems skyward. They love to reach for the sun but, sooner or later, they get top heavy. Even without much of a stiff breeze or a push, they can just keel right over. It makes all the difference in the world for them to have a stake to lean on. It makes all the difference in the world to me, too, to have help when I need it.

Lord, you always hold me up by sending me the help I need—whether it is an encouraging word, a special verse, a friend, or a family member. Whatever I need, you are faithful to give me that stake to lean on. If I pay attention, I realize that it is you supporting me and keeping me going. It is you inspiring someone's heart with what I need.

I don't want to just have a stake, I want to be a stake for someone who needs it. You know what it will take to keep my friend going. You said that we should serve one another with love. Please show me what love looks like to my friend today. Is it a meal? An hour of listening? A hug?

It gives me a happy heart to see my children be good to each other. Surely it pleases you to watch your children be good to each other and help each other over a rough patch. My reward is the joy it gives to me.

YOU HAVE BEEN MY HELP,
THEREFORE IN THE SHADOW OF YOUR WINGS I WILL REJOICE.
MY SOUL FOLLOWS CLOSE BEHIND YOU;
YOUR RIGHT HAND UPHOLDS ME (PSALM 63:7-8, NKJV).

What help have you experienced from the Lord recently?
Are there similar ways in which you could help others?

Talking Disappointments

My disappointments are calling me now and they want to talk to me. In fact, they like to talk to me. They count on finding me willing to listen. They like to repeat the bad things that have happened to me—constantly hitting rewind and play until I can feel the freshness of the pain all over again. They try to stream my losses into my thoughts. Not only do they repeat the past, they exaggerate it and they fudge on the truth. They are trying to destroy my hope that I can get over these disappointments.

The problem with them is that they are spending my time helping me look backward. That orientation dulls my future and my sight of the hope you have for me. I always stumble when I walk backwards.

But now, I'm walking with you and you are taking me forward, teaching me how much bigger your healing power is than any disappointment. You can even heal my memories of these disappointments so that they're nearly forgotten. Written in my mind as if they are written in invisible ink. Written because they did happen, but written so they have no negative impact on my life.

Because you are Truth, you will tell me the truth about the past and about my own heart. You will add back the hope they have subtracted. I choose to fill my thoughts with your words that tell me how to walk forward with you—living out the future you want for me.

I DO NOT REGARD MYSELF AS HAVING LAID HOLD OF IT YET; BUT ONE THING I DO: FORGETTING WHAT LIES BEHIND AND REACHING FORWARD TO WHAT LIES AHEAD, I PRESS ON TOWARD THE GOAL FOR THE PRIZE OF THE UPWARD CALL OF GOD IN CHRIST JESUS (PHILIPPIANS 3:13-14, NASB).

Do you find yourself listening to past disappointments? How can you apply God's truth to those disappointments and see the hope he has for your future?

Butterfly Whiskers

Your intelligence is unfathomable to me. The more scientists discover the intricacies that you have built into your creation, the more astonished I am. Man's sophisticated technology is so primitive up against your workmanship. How easy it is to miss the wonder of a monarch butterfly that flutters and floats in the garden! It looks like fragile, flying stained glass. Yet when this fragile beauty leaves our garden in the fall, it will not go dormant. It will fly all the way to Mexico to escape the cold. How does it know when to leave? How does it find the way?

Scientists have found out about a bit of your handiwork—a 24-hour clock that guides a butterfly's migration. A circadian clock is in the butterfly's antennae—not just in its brain. If the antennae are clipped off, they can no longer navigate by the sun. These two antennae (I call them butterfly "whiskers") are like a special GPS that can keep a butterfly on course for a 2,000 mile migration!

The Proverbs are like that for me: like butterfly whiskers. The book of Proverbs is only one method of guidance you've given me, but it's an important one. These verses of instruction have the ability to keep me on course as I migrate through life. Gently they teach me your way, infuse wisdom into my choices, and help me navigate a beautiful journey. As surely as butterfly whiskers ensure that the butterfly reaches its destination, I hear your voice directing me: "This is the way; walk in it" (Isaiah 30:21).

Trust in the Lord with all your heart,
And lean not on your own understanding;
In all your ways acknowledge Him,
And He shall direct your paths (Proverbs 3:5-6, NKJV).

How does the book of Proverbs help keep you on the right course?
Which verses do you find most challenging?

Lifting My Heart

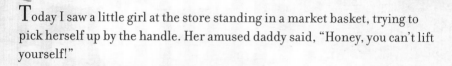

Today I saw a little girl at the store standing in a market basket, trying to pick herself up by the handle. Her amused daddy said, "Honey, you can't lift yourself!"

Lifting myself! I'm surrounded by opportunities to lift myself: lift my success, lift my personality, lighten myself, enlighten myself, even lift my face! A maze of self-improvement strategies, books, internet, infomercials all wanting a newer, better me. "Wouldn't I like a make-over?" they ask. I'm offered so many ways to make-over my appearance, my house, my career, my relationships, my life! It all sounds so exhausting! What a strain!

They got to me too late. I don't need a make-over, Lord Jesus, because you gave me a start-over! When I was able to admit that I was a sinner, I saw that I didn't just act sinfully. Truthfully, my inclination was to disobey you even when I wanted to do better. I couldn't reform my basic nature—I realized I needed a brand new life. I actually needed to be born again and have your life living in me. When I confessed this to you and gave you my life so that you could be the Lord of it, you made me brand new. It was a complete start-over!

Now, your life is in me. You have lifted me out of the hopelessness of living for myself. I truly am lifted. My heart is lifted, my mind is lifted, and yes, even my face is lifted by joy!

ANYONE WHO BELONGS TO CHRIST HAS BECOME A NEW PERSON. THE OLD LIFE IS GONE; A NEW LIFE HAS BEGUN! (2 CORINTHIANS 5:17, NLT)

You can't lift yourself, but God desires to lift all of you: heart, mind, and face! How do you feel about starting over with God?

_____

_____

_____

_____

_____

_____

_____

_____

_____

_____

_____

_____

_____

_____

_____

_____

_____

_____

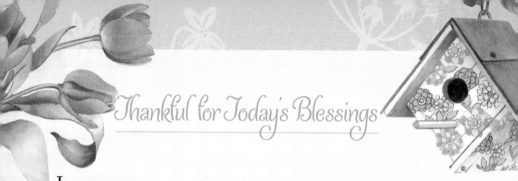

Thankful for Today's Blessings

Lord, I want to thank you for the joys and the provision of today: this very day. There are unknown days ahead, but that uncertainty mustn't distract me from the goodness of this one. Thank you for life, for food, for shelter, for freedom, for family—blessings so constant that I forget to say "thank you" for them. I am surrounded by your goodness and I gather hope from it.

When I consider all you give to me, my glass isn't half empty or half full— it's completely full! My selfishness diminishes and my gratitude increases when I count my blessings and name them one by one. I want to give attention to the basic things: my ability to see and hear, my access to your Word, each day of freedom. None of these things are accidents. They are mine because of your goodness.

If I should lose any—or most—of these blessings? Whatever I had left, I would still have your goodness. Your Word teaches me that I should give thanks to you because you are *good* and your love endures forever. It's not only the blessings I can see and count that I need to offer thanks for, it is for you. What the psalmist said is true for me: "You are my Lord; apart from you I have no good thing" (Psalm 16:2, NIV).

As a preschooler I learned to sing, "God is good." Today I do come before you blessing and praising your name. I am thankful and I want to say so!

GIVE THANKS TO THE LORD, FOR HE IS GOOD;
HIS LOVE ENDURES FOREVER (1 CHRONICLES 16:34, NIV).

Can you see God's goodness in multiple areas of your life?
What are you most thankful for today?

Change

There is always change in the garden. The rose that is unfurled and gorgeous today will lose its petals in only a few days. I cannot hold on to its fleeting beauty. On the other hand, the bud on the same branch would never bloom without change. That is, I suppose, part of the joy of a garden—walking through to delight in what's new.

Change can be refreshing. But change can also be disruptive and it can be unsettling, especially when the change is not my idea. Change in my life is what takes me away from the normal that I'm comfortable with into new normals that aren't quite comfortable. A job change, the loss of a friend, the loss of a parent, the empty nest, or illness can all destroy a comfortable normal. Whether the loss is slow or sudden, once a beloved normal is lost, the way back may be impossible. Life doesn't have a reverse gear—I must go forward and accept my new normal. I can only do that because I know you go with me and you won't ever change.

Even the culture surrounding me has become almost fluid—shifting from your values and the foundations of your Word, Lord, at an increasing tempo. Sometimes change is good. But sometimes change threatens all that is good. What an encouragement it is to wake up every morning and know that you're still the same and that you always will be. Your faithfulness is with me. You are the rock I am building my life on. You refresh me with your love and mercy. You are the hope and confidence of every generation, and you are mine.

For the Lord is good; His mercy *and* loving-kindness are everlasting, His faithfulness *and* truth endure to all generations (Psalm 100:5, amp).

Which changes in your life lately have been refreshing?
Which have been disruptive and unsettling?

Lilies

In the book of Matthew, we're instructed to "Consider the lilies of the field and learn thoroughly how they grow" (Matthew 6:28). Yes, we can study lilies and observe how they grow, yet we don't really know *how* they grow. How did the life get in the bulb? How was a bloom schedule and a growth chart prepackaged in it? I only have to think about a lily to be lost in wonder at your creative power, Lord. How many different lilies are there? Easter lilies, spider lilies, tiger lilies, Lily of the Valley, water lilies—if I could have created one, just one, I would have worldwide attention and acclamation!

I only have to look at the small selection of created flora in my garden to be awestruck at your power and mind. Even those words are woefully inadequate. There are annuals that bloom all summer, then they are gone. There are perennials that don't bloom as long, but are back next year. There are bushes with woody trunks and one that dies back to the ground and starts all over the next year.

Each plant has its own life cycle, reproductive schedule, size, color, seed, likes, and dislikes. The roses are exquisite, yet each variety is different—even the fragrance is as different as blended perfume. The sunflowers turn their faces to the sun while the impatiens relax in the shade. The morning glory vine has only to get close to the trellis and it will wind its way upward.

Can I look at even one of these and doubt that you, who created them and me, can care for me? Lord, please give me a greater capacity for seeing your wonder, your intelligence, and your majesty in everything you have made.

The Lord is good to all,
and His tender mercies are over all His works.
All Your works shall praise You, O Lord,
And Your saints shall bless You (Psalm 145:9-10, nkjv).

Where do you most see the wonder, intelligence, and majesty of the Lord?

_____

_____

_____

_____

_____

_____

_____

_____

_____

_____

_____

_____

_____

_____

_____

_____

_____

_____

_____

_____

The Cross

Although I've always heard of having a cross to bear, Lord, my cross is not a weight of heavy personal burdens that I have to carry around. The cross is where you died and where I, too, come to die. To come in repentance to the cross and receive mercy and forgiveness for my sins is the beginning, the giving of my life to you. To choose death for that part of me that loves to sin is a step further. My self causes me nothing but trouble and there's nothing about it that I want to rescue and keep. Yet, it resists dying. It wants its own way. Always.

I choose the cross for my sin nature so that your resurrected life can live freely in me. Your suffering provided that I am not only free from the sins I've committed, I can be free from being controlled by sin.

Your Word explains that I am crucified with you, but I'm still alive with you living your life in me! The life I now live is lived by faith in you who loved me and gave yourself for me. (See Galatians 2:20.)

I have no words for this kind of love. I can't take credit, Lord, for searching you out and finding you. It was you who came to me when I thought I knew all about you. But I didn't really know you. This love is personal and calls me by my name. How can I ever express the gratitude of my heart?

CONSIDER YOURSELVES TO BE DEAD TO SIN, BUT ALIVE TO GOD IN CHRIST JESUS (ROMANS 6:11, NASB).

Is there sin in your life right now that feels like it is controlling you?
How can you choose to die to this sin and be free?

_____

_____

_____

_____

_____

_____

_____

_____

_____

_____

_____

_____

_____

_____

_____

_____

Conformed to Your Image

In late spring, I like to go out to the garden in the morning to see what the little morning glory plants have been up to during the night. They grow really fast, and it's a wondrous thing to see how the little seedlings reach out to the nearest support as soon as they're tall enough and wrap themselves around it. They cling to the trellis and as they grow all the way up to the top, the vine takes on the trellis shape.

The morning glories make me think of how I reach out to you, Lord. As I let you support and guide me with your Word, I become conformed to your image as my mind is transformed. The morning glories also remind me of how I can lean on your strength, just as they rely on the trellis to hold them up. They end up having the same shape as their support, which I desire too.

You have cautioned me not to be conformed to the world and its superficiality. For that reason, I must be careful about what I focus on and plant my life near. Whatever I stay near to is what I tend to reach out to and lean on. Help me to be wise in my choices so that I am indeed in the world, but not of the world.

To be conformed to your image, I must cling to your cross.

DO NOT CONFORM TO THE PATTERN OF THIS WORLD, BUT BE TRANSFORMED BY THE RENEWING OF YOUR MIND. THEN YOU WILL BE ABLE TO TEST AND APPROVE WHAT GOD'S WILL IS—HIS GOOD, PLEASING AND PERFECT WILL (ROMANS 12:2, NIV).

Do you lean on God for strength?
How do you see yourself taking on his shape as you depend on him?

Loving God

Even though I purposed to love you, Lord, I confess I wondered if I loved you enough and what enough was. When I heard someone say that we tend to love you for what we can get out of you, I was convicted. My love for you did seem to be focused on what I wanted from you: salvation, safety for my family, healing, blessings, prosperity. What did it mean to love you for yourself?

It was your Word that opened my heart to loving you more for yourself. It was when I looked in the book of Psalms to finish this sentence: "You are wonderful because…." and saw what you are to me. Not by reading one verse, but by finishing this sentence over and over as I read the whole book. And you are so wonderful!

You are wonderful because you are the king of glory, my light, my refuge, my salvation, the stronghold of my life. You are the beauty of holiness! You are wonderful because you give me steadfast love, loving-kindness, tender mercy, and strength. You are my rock, my fortress, and my deliverer—worthy of all my trust.

Paying attention to how wonderful you are caused the joy of praise to flow from my heart. There are so many different reasons to praise you—so many ways that you are wonderful! Seeing your heart gave me a love that was all about you instead of a love that was all about me.

I will sing of the mercies of the Lord forever;
With my mouth will I make known Your faithfulness to all generations
(Psalm 89:1, nkjv).

Allow the joy of praise for your God to flow from your heart onto this page.

The Business of Prayer

In the birdbath in the center of our garden, there stands a vintage angel with her head slightly bowed, her arms folded in prayer. I'm not sure that angels actually pray like we do—certainly not concrete ones—but here this angel stands in an attitude of prayer, no matter what else is going on in the garden. Chickadees, somewhat disrespectfully, perch on her head. Other birds bathe and splash at her feet. Squirrels play chase around the base of the birdbath while chipmunks work at digging small craters under the flowers. There's a sense of active cheerful peace, much like my own good days. It's not always summer in the garden though. Sometimes it's cold, windy, and dark. Winter comes. So does night, and so do storms.

Through my own sunny days, nights, and storms, when I look at this molded angel with peeling paint, it is an encouragement to me to remain constantly in an attitude of prayer. If I'm constantly in an attitude of prayer, then I am continually aware of my relationship with you, Lord. Even though the world may swirl around me in activity, true serenity is found in my persistence to pray. My prayer may be full of thankfulness and gratitude or overflowing with praise for who you are. There may be tears for the needs of another or pleading for my own. All of it is in my relationship with you. It is the most important thing that I do. The business of my life is prayer. And it must not be just a part-time business.

PRAY WITHOUT CEASING (1 THESSALONIANS 5:17, NKJV).

How can you incorporate prayer into each waking moment of your day?

Contentment

I've discovered that the more things I thank you for, Lord, the less I want. I first noticed this trend when I was standing in a little antique store trying to choose between a table with carvings of fruit and a table with carvings of flowers. Explaining my indecision to the owner, I told him that I could be happy with either one—or be happy going home with nothing. Expressing heartfelt thanks for each blessing in my life is bringing me an unexpected dividend—contentment.

I once knew someone who had decided that the price of an item was not the determining factor of whether she should buy it. The determining factor was: did you, Lord, want her to have it? She was freed from "is it cheap?" "Is it too expensive?" She just wanted to know if you wanted her to have it.

If I trust you to provide, shouldn't I also trust you to give the right provision for me? What I'm supposed to have has nothing to do with what others have. I don't want to feel envy in my heart toward those who have more. Instead, I want to feel happiness for them. Nor do I want to look down on those with less. Instead, I want to respect them for the labor they do for what they have.

As long as I am diligent in my own labor and responsible in my habits, whether the economy brings feast or famine, I can be content to know that you are my provider and you are constantly providing what is right for me.

DO YOU WANT TO BE TRULY RICH? YOU ALREADY ARE IF YOU ARE HAPPY AND GOOD. AFTER ALL, WE DIDN'T BRING ANY MONEY WITH US WHEN WE CAME INTO THE WORLD, AND WE CAN'T CARRY AWAY A SINGLE PENNY WHEN WE DIE. SO WE SHOULD BE WELL SATISFIED WITHOUT MONEY IF WE HAVE ENOUGH FOOD AND CLOTHING (1 TIMOTHY 6:6-8, TLB).

Express your heartfelt thanks for each blessing in your life.

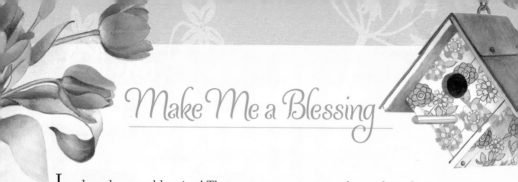

Make Me a Blessing

Lord, make me a blessing! There are so many around me whose lives are begging for a blessing. The needs are so many. There are material needs due to job loss, new or discouraged Christians who need to be nurtured in the faith, family stress, and health challenges. And that is just a basic list! There is much I can do, no, much more than I can do.

My heart is focusing on this prayer: make me a blessing. More than doing things for others that bless them, I'm asking you to make me a blessing. I need to let you control every area of my life so that I am constantly in tune with you. Then the blessings can flow from you, through me, to others. As I continually surrender to your lordship, I surrender my tongue to words that bless and encourage. I'll be grateful for your self-control in me so that I can choose kind silence when no words will help. As I try to maintain a clean heart and pure hands, let your inward presence be noticeable to everyone I come in contact with.

Beyond even that is my desire to be a blessing to you. Instead of focusing on what blessings I would want to beg you for, I want to bless you with my obedience and with my praise, thanking you for everything that you are—calling attention to your goodness. This is my greatest opportunity for ministry!

BLESS THE LORD, O MY SOUL;
AND ALL THAT IS WITHIN ME, BLESS HIS HOLY NAME! (PSALM 103:1, NKJV)

Take a moment to thank God for his goodness.
How can you be a blessing to the Lord and to others?

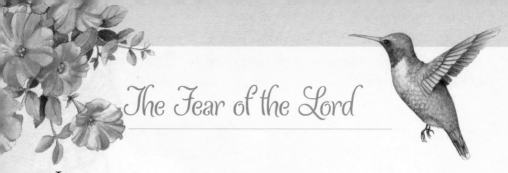

The Fear of the Lord

Lord, I'm saddened to say that this place in time seems to have forgotten how to fear you. Embracing only your love and forgiveness and not all of you robs us of experiencing all that you are. I've been taught that part of fearing you means that I believe you mean what you say. You are as serious about my obedience as you are about blessing me. How can I respond to everything you say in the way you intend if I don't understand and know everything that you are?

It is my heart to walk carefully before you, honoring the truth that you are not only Father, you are also my Lord, my righteousness, my judge, my rock, my fortress, my deliverer, my shield, and so much more. Yes, you are love, mercy, loving-kindness, and graciousness, but you are also my king. As your child, I am under your lordship and authority as well as your care.

Let me never treat you like a buffet where I choose what I like best and pass by what requires my obedience. Rather, I want to pay attention to what you say, and believe that you are all the things you say you are in your Word. I need all of you, and I need to surrender all of me.

As high as the heavens are above the earth,
So great is His lovingkindness toward those who fear Him (Psalm 103:11, nasb).

Do you see God as your king as well as your loving Father?
How can you demonstrate your obedience and love for him today?

Cracked Pot

A bright geranium doesn't seem quite right in a brand new clay pot from the nursery. Somehow, it just looks more comfortable in a cracked pot with a few chips and a little green mold growing on it. It looks, well, *vintage* and has character. I don't like to think of myself as "vintage" or as a "cracked pot," but, Lord, cracks and chips are the way you've been building my character.

Life's disappointments have cracked me. Sometimes the cracks come so quickly and so close together that it almost seems overwhelming. There isn't time to deal and heal with each of them before the next crack is already here. It is my need that keeps me going to your Word, Lord, wanting to see you there and wanting you to use the crack to change me. It is your plan to bring good to me, and if I'm willing to wait and to trust you, you will take advantage of whatever has happened to me. As a result, a deeper confidence in you brings me peace. And joy follows not far behind that.

Yet, I am tempted to wonder how many cracks this little pot can absorb. Instead, though, I consider the hands that hold this pot: hands that allow it to be cracked but never shattered. Let me purpose to better know the heart of your hands so that I may trust your grip and feel secure. I can trust the heart of you, the master, the one who has my name engraved on your hand.

LET HIM HAVE ALL YOUR WORRIES AND CARES, FOR HE IS ALWAYS THINKING ABOUT YOU AND WATCHING EVERYTHING THAT CONCERNS YOU (1 PETER 5:7, TLB).

How do you see the heart of God's hands in his care for you?

_____

_____

_____

_____

_____

_____

_____

_____

_____

_____

_____

_____

_____

_____

_____

_____

_____

_____

Morning

Oh, the gift of a morning with the sun starting to touch the tips of the trees! Such a gift is not to be taken for granted—as I often do—it is the gift of a day. Lord, I'm so grateful that you are depositing another day in my "life account." Opening the door is like stepping into new white leather shoes. There are fresh hours ahead, with no regrets, only possibilities. The morning itself is proof of your faithfulness. The provision that surrounds me is proof of your mercies. Your unfailing love is here as I take up my day.

This new day is time I can spend, but can't save. I start it now by praising you and recognizing your blessings. I let go of yesterday and its problems. And now I lay my requests before you. I surrender my plans to you and ask you to destroy the schemes and plans of the enemy. Help me to walk carefully hour by hour. I ask you to bless your children who are starting this day with difficulties and deprivation. Send help to them, please. Most of all, I want to live this day that way you planned it. You have given this day to me. There will never be another one like it, and I give it back to you as a gift.

THE FAITHFUL LOVE OF THE LORD NEVER ENDS!
HIS MERCIES NEVER CEASE.
GREAT IS HIS FAITHFULNESS;
HIS MERCIES BEGIN AFRESH EACH MORNING (LAMENTATIONS 3:22-23, NLT).

What are you thankful for on this new day?
How can you give this day back to the Lord as a gift?

The Flow of Life

When I see a flower stem or branch that is partly withered or wilted, I look for the fractured or bruised place that has hindered the life flow of the plant. Without that flow, the wounded part of the plant can't maintain the struggle to keep itself vibrant. It wilts or withers. When I see this happen, I want it to be straightened out and restored, to be able to process the flow of life through it and recover.

It's easier to see this process in a wilting plant than it is to acknowledge it in an area of my own life. There are places in my life that are lacking the vibrancy they once had or the vitality they should have. Some of this withering has been some of my own doing. I have to admit that I have been careless about the plumbing in my soul! I do have bent or broken places that are not necessarily wounds from others. They may be places where my own disobedience or negligence has hindered the flow and working of your life in me, Lord.

I'm looking at those places honestly with you, and confessing them as what they are. I'm trusting you to show me everything that has obstructed the full force of your life, love, healing, and mercy from flooding in and through my life. In the scriptures, you healed the withered hand of the man who held it forth to you. I hold all these things forth to you and ask you to heal and cleanse me. It turns out that life is very much a plumbing issue—not only for plants but also for me!

If we confess our sins, he is faithful and just and will forgive us our sins and purify us from all unrighteousness (1 John 1:9, NIV).

Can you identify areas in your life that are lacking the vitality they should have?
What can you do to allow life to flow back into those wilted areas?

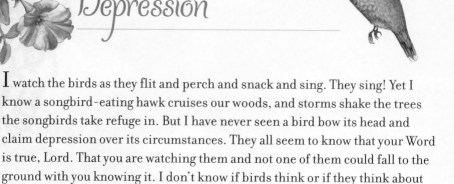

Depression

I watch the birds as they flit and perch and snack and sing. They sing! Yet I know a songbird-eating hawk cruises our woods, and storms shake the trees the songbirds take refuge in. But I have never seen a bird bow its head and claim depression over its circumstances. They all seem to know that your Word is true, Lord. That you are watching them and not one of them could fall to the ground with you knowing it. I don't know if birds think or if they think about their hardships and then choose hope. But I do know that my own thoughts can determine my outlook.

Self-pity would like to enroll me in a class and tutor me on all my injustices, reminding me of everything life has denied me and every hurt I have suffered. In fact, self-pity would like to claim my loyalty as a life time member, causing me to miss your hope entirely!

Discouragement and depression would like to recruit me as well, especially when things don't go my way, keeping me from seeing your ways. They hover near me when I have to face challenges that are in no way my fault.

In order for depression and self-pity to hang their dark clouds over my life, they first have to block me from your presence and the awareness of your goodness. To do that, they would have to keep me from your Word. They can't do that! I am the only one who can keep myself from your Word, where I draw on your hope and find confidence in your character.

The birds are my reminder to refuse self-pity. I will not entertain depression for myself either.

"WHAT IS THE PRICE OF FIVE SPARROWS—TWO COPPER COINS? YET GOD DOES NOT FORGET A SINGLE ONE OF THEM. AND THE VERY HAIRS ON YOUR HEAD ARE ALL NUMBERED. SO DON'T BE AFRAID; YOU ARE MORE VALUABLE TO GOD THAN A WHOLE FLOCK OF SPARROWS" (LUKE 12:6-7, NLT).

You are worth much more to God than many sparrows.
Can you abandon yourself to trust in his care for you just as the songbirds do?

_____

_____

_____

_____

_____

_____

_____

_____

_____

_____

_____

_____

_____

_____

_____

_____

_____

Mr. Fear

There are dark clouds on the horizon, Lord. Clouds that I can't control and may not be able to escape. There are so many things that could go wrong—or wrong*er*—with my family, my work, my city, or my country!

Mr. Fear dropped by to see me today with his portfolio of scenarios for the future. He wanted to help me imagine how frightening my future might be. All of his options at every level were hopeless ones!

Thank you, Lord, for reminding me that I should not entertain Mr. Fear! Mr. Fear is bad company because he takes my thoughts away from you and into imaginary territory. My future is in your hands. Your plans for me are not for calamity, but for a future and a hope. I don't have to know the details right now. I am not and never will be alone. Your Word says that you are with me. I will not be afraid to go forward, for your goodness and your mercy are my constant companions all the days of my life.

My little garden reminds me that life will go on. Some of it will be glorious in abundant blessings, some may feel like winter. But all of it will be my opportunity to trust you, and in all of it I will be thankful for your watchful care.

The birds in my garden are cared for whether I feed them or not. You are their supply. And you are mine.

"Do not fear, for I am with you;
Do not anxiously look about you, for I am your God.
I will strengthen you, surely I will help you,
Surely I will uphold you with My righteous right hand" (Isaiah 41:10, nasb).

Tell Mr. Fear that he cannot make you afraid.
Reflect on how God is your supply and your hope for the future.

The Flowers Fade

As an artist with young children, I used to say that my paintings were one of the few things in my life that were not *undone*. If I cooked a meal, it was eaten and another one needed to be done. If I washed the laundry, in a few days it was all dirty again. Of course it was important to do those tasks so that my family could function.

Even though a garden isn't a chore, it does take constant effort because so much in it is so very temporary: and yes, there are factors that undo those efforts. The weather can change everything. Bugs (or other animals) can eat the plants. Cold weather will, for a time, do most everything in. Yet, it is all worth it for the beauty of the flowers. It is worth it to the hummingbirds and the butterflies for the nourishment they get. For me, it is the fragile, temporary beauty of the flowers that is worth it.

Lord, you use the fragile flowers to make the point that your Word is eternal and will never change. I can count on it—it cannot be undone. Your Word will stand forever. This means that for all future time, you will remain the same. Your promises endure; your truth prevails. You are, as your Word says, my rock in a shifting world. This permanence is the foundation of my hope.

THE GRASS WITHERS, THE FLOWER FADES,
BUT THE WORD OF OUR GOD STANDS FOREVER (ISAIAH 40:8, NKJV).

What things in your life feel as though they are constantly *undone*? Can you see the worth in those things? How does the permanence of God's Word give you hope?

_____
_____
_____
_____
_____
_____
_____
_____
_____
_____
_____
_____
_____
_____
_____
_____
_____
_____
_____
_____
_____

Directions

Being too busy and too optimistic to follow directions has, at times, caused me to approach my garden in a bit of a willy-nilly fashion. Instructions can seem so tedious. Why not just jump in and get started? This plant likes sun? But I like it over here, by the birdbath in a bit of shade. Who knew that bulbs have an up and a down? Both ends will be buried anyway, and the "up" will have to push its way through the dirt, right? And the dirt! Who measures the pH of the soil? Certainly not me.

I don't think of myself as a lawless person (maybe a little careless, but definitely not lawless). When I break the laws of gardening, though, the results are not what I had hoped for. The plants simply can't thrive without my paying attention to the way you made them, Lord, and planned for them to flourish.

Skipping over the directions affects more than my garden; it causes me to examine my heart. Am I really following you, Lord, by paying careful attention to your instructions? Do I shy away from the red letter words because those can be hard things to obey? Am I making it up as I go along, thinking all will be well as long as I mean well? If I do that, my results will not be any better than the results in my garden.

Help me to slow down and carefully read your Word with a willing and obedient heart. Help me to think of the words as instructions—not suggestions. Only by following your directions can I participate in fulfilling your purposes for me.

Your word is a lamp to guide my feet
and a light for my path (Psalm 119:105, nlt).

What directions in God's Word do you sometimes skip over? Do you see how those
directions are there to help you fulfill the purpose God has for you?

My Pain

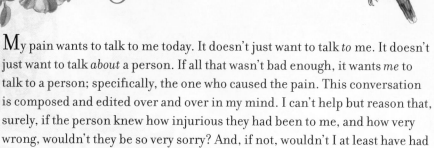

My pain wants to talk to me today. It doesn't just want to talk *to* me. It doesn't just want to talk *about* a person. If all that wasn't bad enough, it wants *me* to talk to a person; specifically, the one who caused the pain. This conversation is composed and edited over and over in my mind. I can't help but reason that, surely, if the person knew how injurious they had been to me, and how very wrong, wouldn't they be so very sorry? And, if not, wouldn't I at least have had my say? Wouldn't I have given them a chance to own what they did?

The problem is these chats that my pain is helping me compose not only remind, they also accuse the other person. Am I allowed to confront with truth? Sometimes, yes. But do you allow me to accuse? No. Our enemy is the accuser and accusations are guaranteed to cause trouble. It is not for me to determine whether the pain caused was careless or intentional. If I let my pain have its way and speak, then I become the one who is causing more pain!

I'm not to accuse, but your Holy Spirit can convict and convince in a way that I never could. I need to put this in your hands. I cannot trust my pain, but I choose to trust you to somehow work this to my good. I want the words of my mouth and the meditation of my heart to be acceptable to you. I want that more than I want to have my say.

LOVE BEARS UP UNDER ANYTHING *AND* EVERYTHING THAT COMES, IS EVER READY TO BELIEVE THE BEST OF EVERY PERSON, ITS HOPES ARE FADELESS UNDER ALL CIRCUMSTANCES, AND IT ENDURES EVERYTHING [WITHOUT WEAKENING] (1 CORINTHIANS 13:7, AMP).

In what ways is your pain trying to justify unforgiveness and anger?
What can you do to show that you trust God to convince and convict where needed?

_____

_____

_____

_____

_____

_____

_____

_____

_____

_____

_____

_____

_____

_____

_____

_____

_____

_____

_____

_____

The Woodpecker

The woodpecker relentlessly pecks at the largest branch of my helpless, hapless rose bush, not thinking it may interrupt its very life. A bandage of blue electrical tape wrapped around the wound is not, alas, an adequate barrier of protection against this persistent woodpecker.

Like the woodpecker, my enemy, Satan, likes to peck and peck at my mind. He aims to keep me busy with accusations, assigning motives, speculations, and out and out lies—anything but the truth! Listening to his lies only gives him an opportunity to tell me more lies. All of it is designed to hinder and harm my destiny as your child, Lord, by instigating sin against you and others. It also wastes my time and energy.

Blue tape is not an effective barrier against the woodpecker, but truth is a powerful barrier between me and the enemy's pecking. You are the barrier of truth to protect my mind. Your Word is truth to saturate my mind. I need a daily dose of your Word to systematically build layer after layer in my truth barrier. The enemy has no defense against truth. Besides protecting me from being deceived, your truth is an unchanging stability for me in a changing world. For truth is what is real. Truth is never relative; truth is you.

STAND YOUR GROUND, PUTTING ON THE BELT OF TRUTH AND THE BODY ARMOR OF GOD'S RIGHTEOUSNESS (EPHESIANS 6:14, NLT).

What truths or promises in God's Word help you protect your mind from the pecking of the enemy? How can you be sure to saturate your mind with truth?

_____

_____

_____

_____

_____

_____

_____

_____

_____

_____

_____

_____

_____

_____

_____

_____

_____

_____

_____

_____

_____

_____

Discernment

More and more I see that to really *love* you, Lord, I need to really *know* you. And to serve you, it's increasingly important to me to discern what is like you and what isn't. I've heard the recommendation that to truly love a person, you must study them and notice their likes and dislikes. You have to find out what's important to them.

I wonder if that wisdom was inspired by Ephesians 5:10: "Find out what pleases the Lord" (NIV).

How can I live with proper love for you if I don't pay attention to what pleases you and if I don't know you well enough to know what grieves you? I want to be sensitive to recognize your working and your presence—what is of you and what isn't. Holy Spirit, please alert my heart to anything that is offensive to you. As I read your Word, point out to me what is like you and what isn't. Your first commandment is to love you with all my heart, with all my soul, with all my mind, and with all my strength.

"'LOVE THE LORD YOUR GOD WITH ALL YOUR HEART, WITH ALL YOUR SOUL, WITH ALL YOUR MIND, AND WITH ALL YOUR STRENGTH.' THIS IS THE FIRST COMMANDMENT" (MARK 12:30, NKJV).

What does loving God look like in your current situation?
What do you think would be pleasing to the Lord?

_____

_____

_____

_____

_____

_____

_____

_____

_____

_____

_____

_____

_____

_____

_____

_____

_____

My Self

It was about midnight when I heard, "Eeek!" It was the cry of an animal in trouble. By the time I got downstairs, the damage had been done. A little rabbit lay wounded on the ground, unable to get up. The predator's first blow had been a serious one. Was it a coyote, or a hawk? A stroke of a broad, grey wing came across the window. An owl. Owls have a beauty of their own and enjoy a lot of popularity. But the truth is it is the nature of an owl to dine on cute woodland animals.

As a human being, I too have a nature that isn't very attractive. It is my *self*. The nature of self is to always want its own way, not yours, Lord. I struggle with it, trying to get it to behave as a Christian, but it cannot be reformed. Even if I dress it up and put lipstick on it—it is what it is. It is still selfish. You solved this hopeless conundrum for me when you took my self to the cross and ended its domination and power over me.

As long as I choose death for this self, I enjoy the freedom of having your life flow through me, expressing itself in my personality. There really isn't anything about this selfish willfulness that I want to rescue. Everything good that I want is in you! Thank you for freeing me from the discouragement of trying to rehabilitate what is my nature, and instead giving me the miracle of replacing it with your nature.

HE DIED ONCE FOR ALL TO END SIN'S POWER, BUT NOW HE LIVES FOREVER IN UNBROKEN FELLOWSHIP WITH GOD. SO LOOK UPON YOUR OLD SIN NATURE AS DEAD AND UNRESPONSIVE TO SIN, AND INSTEAD BE ALIVE TO GOD, ALERT TO HIM, THROUGH JESUS CHRIST OUR LORD (ROMANS 6:10-11, TLB).

Who is winning your fight with self?
How can you find freedom in surrendering to Christ?

Thirst

In the woods where we live, a small herd of deer is completely at ease meandering past our home. We usually see five together, but there may be more. The seasons are marked with the addition of fawns, but who knows how many we lose to the coyotes? Although they have been known to shamelessly plunder our flower bed and the birdfeeder if we're away, mostly they trot by, seeming to be not in the least tempted by the snacks in our yard. With an occasional flash of white tails, the young follow the old as they bound or stroll down the trail—driven to the creek by their thirst.

The psalmist compared his own thirst for you, Lord, to the panting of the deer for the stream of water. (See Psalm 42:1.) and it's a good picture of my own thirst as well. There was a time when thirst for other things masked my real thirst. Education, career, family, and recognition all pulled me toward more and more, but all of it had a taste that never satisfied. When I surrendered my life to you, I truly found living water that quenched all the thirst of my life.

Though I may get distracted with work, activity, and thoughts about other things, none of that can satisfy my thirst for you, your presence, and your words. You created me to have this thirst that can only be satisfied by your very life living in me.

"Whoever drinks of the water that I shall give him will never thirst. But the water that I shall give him will become in him a fountain of water springing up into everlasting life" (John 4:14, nkjv).

Can you identify things that you are thirsty for that might be masking your thirst for God? How can you be satisfied by the living water?

Discouragement

Discouragement is following me everyday. Dogging my steps. Daily. It only has one thing to say: "Quit!" But quit what? Life is so intertwined. How do I quit the hard part and keep the pleasant, happy parts? Lord, I don't remember seeing "quit" in your Word, or "give up," but I'm not sure how I can go on. I'm not sure how to quit either! Exactly where does one go to resign? Discouragement wants to intimidate me, assuring me that I won't know how to go forward—that I don't have the strength.

As long as I can breathe, life must go on, but where is the strength, the wisdom, the courage? I am weary, Lord. Your Word talks about hiding me under your wings, about being a strong tower that I can run into and be safe. Your Word also talks about standing. I can stand in my place while you support me.

In the spring, my climbing rose almost smothers the arbor in fragrant pink blooms, but as I look at it now, in winter, it looks a lot like me. A few dead branches, a wound from an aggressive woodpecker, a broken limb. But it is standing! Waiting for the life within it to bring spring.

Right now, what it's doing is not very impressive. But cuttings from just one heirloom rose can carry forth beauty and fragrance of that rose for over a hundred years in multiplied places. Lord, I'm not going to quit. I'm going to stand—stand right here in my place and trust you to do in me what it takes to carry forth your fragrance into my future.

I WAITED PATIENTLY FOR THE LORD;
HE TURNED TO ME AND HEARD MY CRY.
HE LIFTED ME OUT OF THE SLIMY PIT,
OUT OF THE MUD AND MIRE;
HE SET MY FEET ON A ROCK
AND GAVE ME A FIRM PLACE TO STAND (PSALM 40:1-2, NIV).

How do you sense the Lord making your life a beautiful fragrance
in spite of the hardships you go through?

_____

_____

_____

_____

_____

_____

_____

_____

_____

_____

_____

_____

_____

_____

_____

_____

_____

_____

My Tongue

It's true that no person can tame the tongue. It's not that it has a mind of its own, but that the mind that operates it isn't always under your control, Lord. Oh, how many things I wish I had not spoken! My tongue has caused more trouble than I want to own, but I don't want my misuse of it to cause me to miss what a wonderful instrument it is.

Lord, I'm shifting my focus from how not to use my tongue to how to please you with it. Amazing in design, it gives voice to my heart. It lets me speak and sing. The songwriter wished for a thousand tongues to sing your praises! I can sing your praises and speak forth the wonder of your deeds and the glory of your character. I can speak your Word. My tongue can share my testimony of who you are and what you have done for me. My tongue can share comfort with someone who is hurting and encouragement for someone who is struggling. It can point out the good and celebrate your blessings. And, when it is appropriate, it can gently reprove.

At a cue from you, it can even be still—choosing quiet when quiet is much better than words. Under your control, my tongue can be a continual blessing—with no time to cause grief from mindless chat and careless words. Lord, my tongue can be tamed by you. I'm offering you control of my tongue!

PLEASANT WORDS ARE LIKE A HONEYCOMB,
SWEETNESS TO THE SOUL AND HEALTH TO THE BONES (PROVERBS 16:24, NKJV).

What are some ways you can use your tongue to please God?

_____

_____

_____

_____

_____

_____

_____

_____

_____

_____

_____

_____

_____

_____

_____

_____

_____

Walking

It's interesting to watch the nuthatches walk up and down the side of the tree. They remind me a little of Fred Astaire dancing on the ceiling. It seems a little gravity-defying for them to walk vertically on the tree, stashing little seed snacks to pick up later. But that's the walk they've been given.

Lord, your Word says a lot about my walk and how I should walk. Walking seems symbolic of the business of life—the idea of moving forward. Habakkuk 3:19 says, "The Lord God is my Strength, my personal bravery, and my invincible army; He makes my feet like hinds' feet and will make me to walk [not to stand still in terror, but to walk] and make [spiritual] progress upon my high places [of trouble, suffering, or responsibility]!" (AMP)

I am expected to make spiritual progress in my life whether I have trouble, suffering, or just daily responsibility. How am I to walk in your ways of truth, light, love, and wisdom? You are all of these things. You are truth, you are light, you are love, and you are wisdom. I invite you to be truth, light, love, and wisdom in my life so that my walk will truly look like you.

Just as you have made the nuthatch well-suited to his way of walking, you have empowered me with your Holy Spirit to be able to walk humbly in your ways as you show them to me.

He has shown you, O man, what is good;
And what does the Lord require of you
But to do justly,
To love mercy,
And to walk humbly with your God? (Micah 6:8, nkjv)

How does your walk reflect God's truth, light, love, and wisdom?

Failing

I always wanted to be the best and the brightest: the one who did well. But by the time I could process how great it would be to be perfect, I already wasn't. Failure isn't something we talk about much. In women's groups, nobody seems to raise their hand and say, "I've failed." But I think a lot may feel that way. How many of us have it all? How many actually look like models, are wildly successful at their jobs, have the perfect house and home life, and—on top of that—are living authentic Christian lives? Not many of us would give ourselves a perfect 10.

Lord, everything I've considered a failure, I bring to the cross and leave it there. Where there was sin, I repent and turn from it. Where someone else failed me, I forgive. I refuse to be defined by other people's expectations or definitions of success. I'm determined that my heart will be faithful and focused on you.

Your Word reassures me that you never fail. Your love never fails. I can always count on your faithfulness. Failure is about disappointing you, who loves me and created me, by focusing on my own circumstances so much that I never take time to know you.

Matthew 1:21 says that Jesus will save his people from their sins and "prevent them from failing and missing the true end and scope of life, which is God" (AMP). The great opportunity of my life is not to have perfect circumstances. The great opportunity of my life is to personally know you.

"BE STRONG AND COURAGEOUS. DO NOT BE AFRAID OR TERRIFIED BECAUSE OF THEM, FOR THE LORD YOUR GOD GOES WITH YOU; HE WILL NEVER LEAVE YOU NOR FORSAKE YOU" (DEUTERONOMY 31:6, NIV).

Consider what you feel are your failures.
Can you see God's faithfulness at work in you? How do you think God truly sees you?

Open My Eyes

In the freshness of the morning, I almost missed it: a brief glimmer of a gossamer medallion, like a disk of silken lace stretched between the flowers. I looked again and it was gone—or was it? Again it caught the light. An intricate spider web with just the right tension to neither break nor sag. Surprised by its beauty, for a moment I was caught in the wonder of it.

Open my eyes, Lord! What other marvels of your creation do I walk past not seeing? Flowers don't offer the only beauty in the garden. Am I truly looking at everything around me, or merely scanning?

How open are my eyes when I open my Bible? What wondrous things do I miss when I read your Word? Am I reading with understanding or am I merely scanning? I love reading the truths that are familiar and the verses that are my favorites. Part of my Bible is well-worn where my fingerprints have soiled the pages. Truths I want to remember are underlined in blue ink. Notes are scribbled in the margins.

What is troubling me now, Lord, is the clean pages. The pages that are rarely, if ever, read, much less underlined. The question is, what am I missing that you want me to see? None of your Word is outdated. You have given all of it because I need all of it. Open my eyes and my heart to see everything you have for me.

OPEN MY EYES, THAT I MAY SEE
WONDROUS THINGS FROM YOUR LAW (PSALM 119:18, NKJV).

How open are your eyes to the marvels of creation?
How open are they to the wonders written in God's Word?

_____

_____

_____

_____

_____

_____

_____

_____

_____

_____

_____

_____

_____

_____

_____

_____

_____

_____

_____

Wasting Blessings

It is with amusement that I watch the birds at our feeder. The chickadees, gold finches, and sparrows flutter about for position.
Their little beaks work like shovels, and as they rake the seeds out,
they fall in spurts of seed showers. They go at it as if they were looking
for the blue M & M!

Meanwhile on the ground, a contented group of doves, chipmunks, squirrels, and cardinals munch on the leftovers. As I watch the little birds run through their blessings in a willy-nilly fashion, I wonder,
Do I do that?

Lord, when you send me abundance (really more than I need), do I go through it with a willy-nilly abandonment? Am I wasteful? Do I take your blessings for granted? Awash in the joy of my resources, do I even remember to thank you? Is my contentment dial set at maximum blessings? Am I eager to share my fresh blessings or just the leftovers that I no longer want?

Please forgive me when I neglect to truly appreciate your generous provisions. I don't want to wastefully take them for granted. I thank you for every daily blessing—my shelter, my food, my clothes, my family—they are more than I can name. They are all from your hand. From your own heart, I ask you to give me generosity toward others.

Enter his gates with thanksgiving;
go into his courts with praise.
Give thanks to him and praise his name.
For the Lord is good.
His unfailing love continues forever,
and his faithfulness continues to each generation (Psalm 100:4-5, nlt).

Do you find yourself taking the Lord's blessings for granted?
Spend some time appreciating him for all he has given you.

_____

_____

_____

_____

_____

_____

_____

_____

_____

_____

_____

_____

_____

_____

_____

_____

_____

_____

_____

Feeding the Birds

Even though we live in the woods, I never gave much thought to the birds until we hung up a bird feeder. It just hung there a day or two…then *bingo!* Here were the birds! Colorful, beautiful birds I had never noticed before—chickadees, nuthatches, goldfinches—and all of them apparently famished! They swooped from the trees, fluttered for position at the feeder, and snacked off the ground. We felt so good to be feeding them!

Then one day, the feeder was empty and the garden was still and quiet. That's when we learned: food here equaled birds here. Food gone equaled birds gone. The curious thing was that when they returned to a replenished buffet, they didn't look like they had missed a meal. Their feathers weren't loose. They didn't seem to have dropped a size.

Why? Because you, Lord, are feeding them all the time. The truth is they don't really need us. They do perfectly well without us. It makes us feel good to feed them, but it is you that they depend on. We are only a bonus.

I can't help but see myself in these birds. So many times I look to the bonus blessings of my life whether those are new opportunities, new clients, or a bigger check, and I flutter around them. For a moment, I may be slow to recognize that it is not my networking and business savvy but you who is providing for me both in special ways and in everyday ways. Behind the scenes it is you who is giving me what I need, as you do the birds, in ways I never see. Your Word says that you are giving to me, even in my sleep. With all my heart, I thank you for your faithfulness.

Bless the Lord, O my soul,
And forget not all His benefits (Psalm 103:2, NKJV).

Can you see God behind the many blessings in your life?
Take a moment to write down all the special ways he has provided for you.

Opportunities

Life is always looking for an opportunity. Grass knows no boundaries! Even a flower that looks so fragile has the nerve to push itself through in the unlikeliest places, determined to thrive in inhospitable places. We see them proudly standing there between bricks and in sidewalk cracks. Hollyhocks are like that. If only I could be like them!

When I got my first shoots of hollyhocks from the mail-order nursery, I wondered if they were here to stay or a one-year wonder. Not to worry—before long, it was "here a hollyhock, there hollyhock, everywhere a hollyhock!" In with the lilies, under the roses, between the bricks in the walk, seeds of hollyhock life had definitely found opportunity. It didn't look like they missed any opportunity to plant a seed. I want to be a hollyhock, not missing any opportunity to share who you are, Lord, and why you're important in my life.

But the environment I live in seems more and more resistant to plantings of faith. My surroundings include some hard hearts and conflicting minds-all with deep need of hope. Comfortable conversations about you don't always come easily. Words that seem like a good idea to me fall like duds. But even hearts that on the surface appear to be made of concrete cannot resist the power of your life when the words are prompted by you.

Please design opportunities for me where I may cast seeds of your life as I go. Prompt me to see them so that I don't miss them. Help me to be faithful and consistent in sharing what I know of you—even in places that would seem to be inhospitable. Put your words in my mouth when I need them, and I will trust you to bring forth life from those seeds.

Everyone enjoys a fitting reply;
it is wonderful to say the right thing at the right time! (Proverbs 15:23, NLT)

Are you determined to thrive spiritually even in inhospitable places?
What can you do to be faithful and consistent in sharing God's goodness with others?

_____

_____

_____

_____

_____

_____

_____

_____

_____

_____

_____

_____

_____

_____

_____

_____

_____

_____

Watching You

We have sparrows in our garden, and I have to admit they're not the first birds my eyes go to. In fact, I rarely watch them at all, preferring to look at the more colorful birds. But your Word, Lord, says that you watch them and that if even one of them falls, you know it. When I try to comprehend that by multiplying all the birds by all the gardens and telephone wires in the world, your greatness is beyond my imagining. I could never watch even all the sparrows in my garden, but you watch them all. And you've promised me that I don't need to fear; I am worth more to you than many sparrows. Nothing happens to me that you don't see. You watch me very carefully.

When I'm going through something I can't figure out, it's so hard for me to see how you're working and what you're doing while I'm concentrating on myself. I start straining to see what your hands are doing, when what I really need to do is watch you so that I can see your heart. You reveal yourself in your Word so that I can have a place to look where I can be certain that I will see you.

When I face a challenge, what is it that you want to show me about yourself that I've never see before? There is something about watching you that reassures me that you're watching me.

THE LORD IS WATCHING HIS CHILDREN, LISTENING TO THEIR PRAYERS; BUT THE LORD'S FACE IS HARD AGAINST THOSE WHO DO EVIL (1 PETER 3:12, TLB).

What have you missed seeing by focusing on your circumstances instead of God?

Forgiveness

The garden is asleep for the winter and has traded its colors for neutrals. There is a beauty in the quiet winter landscape. Branches are like wooden lace. Trees are showing the strength of their skeleton-like structures. It would almost be pretty except for the dried stalk in the ground that is bending, but not broken. I could cut it down; it is a bit of an eyesore. Yet it is useful to the birds as they light there and perch.

Sadly, I confess there's a dead stalk in my heart too. It's unforgiveness over a past hurt. I wonder if I haven't pulled it out by the roots yet because the stalk is handy. Too handy. For it is there my blame and unhappy memories perch. How do I remove this painful stalk—the memory of something that really did happen? How can I forgive those who wronged me and caused me hurt and loss? My sense of justice can't say, "Oh, it's okay," because I know it wasn't okay and it wasn't right. Nevertheless, I want my life to be defined by love not by a grudge. Lord, you command me to forgive, but what does that look like?

You offer me a detailed blueprint in 1 Corinthians 13 for building my life on love. It has definite instructions for your designed response to those who have wounded me. Your Word says that love "takes no account of the evil done to it [it pays no attention to a suffered wrong] (1 Corinthians 13:5, AMP). I can only do that if I am willing to give up my rights to any kind of apology or revenge.

At first thought, that plan seems to expect way too much of me—the victim—but then I realize how perfectly right it is. It is the kind of love that I so desperately need. It is the response I need from you and others that I offend. My own response to those who cause me pain must be nothing less.

LOVE IS PATIENT AND KIND. LOVE IS NOT JEALOUS OR BOASTFUL OR PROUD OR RUDE.
IT DOES NOT DEMAND ITS OWN WAY. IT IS NOT IRRITABLE, AND IT KEEPS NO
RECORD OF BEING WRONGED (1 CORINTHIANS 13:5, NLT).

Can you identify people in your life who need your forgiveness?
How can you be defined by love instead of by a grudge?

Ownership

I am yours, Lord. I cannot question your ownership. You clearly state it in your Word: the earth is yours, and everything in it belongs to you! (See Psalm 24:1.) That pretty much covers it. You are Lord and creator of everything. Yet, in all the earth and creation, in spite of your magnificence and omnipotence, only *people* resist your ownership. In your wisdom, you let us choose life with you—or life without you.

Even though I call the children I gave birth to "my" children, in a sense, they really don't have a choice about being my children until they are adults. Then they have the option to choose to love me for myself. When they choose to love me and spend time with me, the parent-child relationship becomes even richer as it morphs into lifelong friends of the heart.

Would you want less from me than I want from my children? I don't believe that you've given me the choice to know you just because you want my allegiance. It's your Father's heart that wants me to know your love and your ways. Your heart wants me to resemble you. It's your heart that wants me to want to be your child and desire to spend time with you—to love you not for a balance sheet of blessings, but for yourself.

SEE HOW VERY MUCH OUR FATHER LOVES US, FOR HE CALLS US HIS CHILDREN, AND THAT IS WHAT WE ARE! BUT THE PEOPLE WHO BELONG TO THIS WORLD DON'T RECOGNIZE THAT WE ARE GOD'S CHILDREN BECAUSE THEY DON'T KNOW HIM (1 JOHN 3:1, NLT).

How can you ensure that when people look at you, they see that you belong to God?

Your Hands

Lord, I try so hard to see your hands and to figure out how you are working and what you are doing. How are you working in the background of my life, my church, and the whole world? We used to sing a catchy little song about the world being in your hands. And, of course, it is. In the book of Colossians, it says that your power holds everything together.

From my point of view, though, things don't look like they're going very well. The world stage right now certainly doesn't seem like anything you would set up. In fact, on many levels it looks like things are spinning out of control. If what I can see and what I can understand was the final story, my hope right now would be running low. But your ways and how your hands are working in this world are beyond my understanding and my ability to calculate. I confess that I don't have the wisdom to see your larger purposes. You work in ways I can't possibly see. My hope is secured in what you have told me about yourself:

"For My thoughts are not your thoughts,
Nor are your ways My ways," declares the Lord.
"For as the heavens are higher than the earth,
So are My ways higher than your ways
And My thoughts than your thoughts.
For as the rain and the snow come down from heaven,
And do not return there without watering the earth
And making it bear and sprout,
And furnishing seed to the sower and bread to the eater;
So will My word be which goes forth from My mouth;
It will not return to Me empty,
Without accomplishing what I desire,
And without succeeding in the matter for which I sent it" (Isaiah 55:8-11, nasb).

For this reason, I know that I am praying correctly for things I don't understand, and certainly can't control, when I agree with you. Your will be done. In all things, I pray that your will may be moved from heaven to earth. You do, indeed, have the whole world in your hands.

What can you agree with God for today?

Garden Choices

My perennial springtime question is "What shall I put in my garden?" What colors will I splash onto this blank canvas? So many decisions! Tall, short, perennial, annual, shade, sun, partial sun! My garden is bordered by roses—antique roses that have learned to survive well by forgiving those who neglect them. But in the center, around the birdbath, I start over every year.

This year, salvia, geraniums, hollyhocks, petunias, and even butterfly weed are strategic in my mission to attract hummingbirds and butterflies. If all goes well, this year my garden will both hum and flutter. And I must have my familiar old faces: zinnias, verbena, sunflowers, and daisies.

So, how does my garden grow? With my favorite things! Space is limited and I fill it carefully with beauty that delights me every morning. My pleasure in it is dependent on how selective I am. In the same way, your pleasure, Lord, and my own well-being are dependent on what I select to put in my life. Not only are there destructive things, there are *good* things that can push your choices right out.

Lord, my heart wants to make the choices that will fill my life with your favorite things. Thank you for your Word and the way it teaches me what you desire in my life. Please guide me as I make purposeful decisions about what to add and what to leave out. It is my desire to live the life that you have already planned just for me. I want you to be both pleased and delighted to see the beauty of faith, hope, and love growing in me.

DO NOT BE DECEIVED, GOD IS NOT MOCKED; FOR WHATEVER A MAN SOWS, THAT HE WILL ALSO REAP (GALATIANS 6:7, NKJV).

What do you think are a few of God's favorite things?
What does he desire for your life?

_____

_____

_____

_____

_____

_____

_____

_____

_____

_____

_____

_____

_____

_____

_____

_____

Pests

How frustrating it is to carefully plant a neat little garden and then come back to find that it has become a bug buffet and a snack bar for critters! I'm finding out that by careful selection I can make my garden more resistant to pests. In a marvelous way, Lord, you have provided some natural protections for the garden by making certain plants resist pests and others attract helpful insects. You not only created marigolds to lend hardy cheer, they're also designed to repel aphids and at least two kinds of beetles. Bachelor buttons, my favorite blue flowers, attract helpful insects that go after the bad guys. My garden doesn't need to be a defenseless target for pests—and neither does my life!

Lord, if I pay attention to cultivating the things you want in my life, pests won't have much of a chance. There's not much room for selfishness to grow in a giving heart. Lies can't take root as long as I'm committed to absolute truth. Diligence leaves no time for laziness. Love doesn't give unkindness a chance. Hope pushes out discouragement. Doubt withers in the presence of faith. Determined obedience keeps sin from sprouting. Gentleness leaves no ground for anger. A humble heart has no room for pride.

The next time a pest attacks my life, please show me, Lord, what I specifically need to cultivate in my heart so that particular sin can't do damage in my life.

THE HOLY SPIRIT PRODUCES THIS KIND OF FRUIT IN OUR LIVES: LOVE, JOY, PEACE, PATIENCE, KINDNESS, GOODNESS, FAITHFULNESS, GENTLENESS, AND SELF-CONTROL. THERE IS NO LAW AGAINST THESE THINGS! (GALATIANS 5:22-23, NLT)

What "pests" linger around your life? How can you cultivate a pest-free heart?

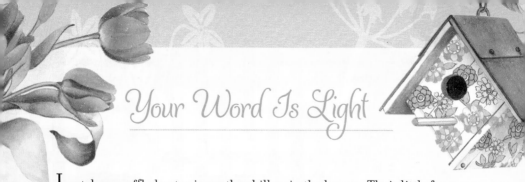

Your Word Is Light

I watch my ruffled petunias as they billow in the breeze. Their little faces always seem to want to face the sun. On sunny days and on cloudy days, their orientation is toward the sun—in May and even into the fall. The sun is not only warmth and light, it is life for them: an essential part of their very photosynthesis process. Without consistent light, the growth petunias have is stunted, and the beauty you designed in them is subnormal, Lord.

You give me light from your Word as I follow your heart. This is my stability in sunny days and cloudy days as I set my face toward you. Day by day I can see a little bit more of your heart. Dose by dose, this vital knowledge is built into my life. If I put my petunias in my basement, away from the light, it would be a little while before they began to droop, but droop they would. If I neglect your Word for a few days, it seems that I can coast for a while, but not for long. Before too many days, my spirit feels cloudy and I, too, am drooping without my daily light.

It is by the reading of your Word that I can know the feelings and purposes of your heart in my own heart. Thank you for making your light shine on my path and in my heart.

For God, who said, "Let there be light in the darkness," has made this light shine in our hearts so we could know the glory of God that is seen in the face of Jesus Christ (2 Corinthians 4:6, nlt).

How do you feel when you neglect the light of God's Word?
What's a common Scripture you go to when you need encouragement?

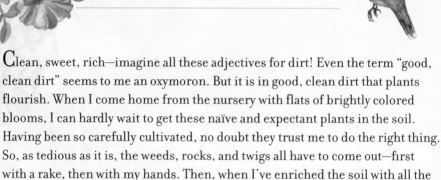

Good Dirt

Clean, sweet, rich—imagine all these adjectives for dirt! Even the term "good, clean dirt" seems to me an oxymoron. But it is in good, clean dirt that plants flourish. When I come home from the nursery with flats of brightly colored blooms, I can hardly wait to get these naïve and expectant plants in the soil. Having been so carefully cultivated, no doubt they trust me to do the right thing. So, as tedious as it is, the weeds, rocks, and twigs all have to come out—first with a rake, then with my hands. Then, when I've enriched the soil with all the needed nutrients, the new home is ready for the plants.

Spilled gravel here, stray branch fragments there—it's easy for debris to accumulate in my garden. And the truth is it's easy for debris to accumulate in my heart, too. Picking out all this debris makes me want a clean heart even more than a clean garden. I confess to you, Lord, that harsh words, grudges, and old hurts litter the soil of my heart.

Forgive me for expecting your Word to bring forth its intended harvest when the soil of my heart is neither good nor clean. Show me every stone, bad root, and bitter seed that has found a home in my heart. Expose the hard places I don't even see. I will throw all of this trash out and refuse to let it litter my soul any longer. I will plant your Word in good soil that it will bring forth an abundance of the fruit of your Spirit in my life.

"The seed falling on good soil refers to someone who hears the word and understands it. This is the one who produces a crop, yielding a hundred, sixty or thirty times what was sown" (Matthew 13:23, niv).

What can you do to make sure you have good soil in your heart?
How does this bring forth an abundance of good fruit?

_____

_____

_____

_____

_____

_____

_____

_____

_____

_____

_____

_____

_____

_____

_____

_____

Pride

Lord, I need to talk with you about pride—my pride. You see, I have liked my pride, and it would seem that my pride likes me! It is always on my side, wants me to be right, wants me to have the best, and works hard to keep my image. It also does its best to cover me when I'm wrong, helps me fight for what I deserve, and protects me from ever being humbled. When it's at its best, I never have to compromise, and I never have to apologize even when my judgment is clouded and I am clearly wrong.

But is it really my friend? In the mirror of your Word, I am painfully aware that pride doesn't deal in the truth. And the truth is that my pride is not working for me because it isn't like you.

In my world, self-image and self-confidence are big buzz words. But *self* (which must be short for selfishness)—that thing that loves and promotes *me* above all else—is what you took to the cross. You suffered so that I could be free from it. You chose death for me. If I choose death to self, then I am in *your* image and my confidence is in *you*.

It would seem that something that was always on my side, always looking out for me, would be my friend, but it's not. It is my enemy. I'm beginning to see why pride is one of the seven deadly sins! It hinders my relationship with you because it's sin, and it troubles my relationships with others. With all my heart, Lord, I do choose humility and the relief of not having to defend myself, accuse others, or expect others to perform for me. Pride didn't want me to see this…or to see you as you are. Thank you for showing it to me.

Pride leads to disgrace,
but with humility comes wisdom (Proverbs 11:2, nlt).

Have you recognized pride as your enemy?
What does it look like to choose humility instead of pride?

Growth

The ups and downs of the economy won't stop the turn of the seasons. The bad news of the day cannot hold back spring. Even wars—or rumors of war—will not keep the life within the bulb of the lily from pushing it up through the dirt and unfurling its petals into a dazzling trumpet. Neither could a recession keep the vine of roses from leafing out and releasing its fragrance in a mass of delicate blooms. Nor can difficult circumstances hinder the unstoppable work of your Spirit in my life, Lord.

What really matters is not what's happening in the world around me. What matters is the climate of my own heart. When I keep an attitude of submission and devotion to you, Lord, my heart is a peaceful, fruitful place for you to dwell and work your purposes. You have promised to perfect the good work you have begun in me. I must not lag behind, waiting until there is nothing but good news in my circumstances, before I yield everything to you with a whole heart.

If I put all my trust, hope, and confidence in you, your Word says I will be like a tree planted by waters that will have green leaves and won't fear when heat comes. In a year of drought, I won't be anxious or full of care, nor will I cease yielding fruit. (See Jeremiah 17:7-8.)

Please, Lord, water my heart and soul with hope and confidence in you that I may, like that tree, bear much fruit—regardless of the times.

FOR I AM CONFIDENT OF THIS VERY THING, THAT HE WHO BEGAN A GOOD WORK IN YOU WILL PERFECT IT UNTIL THE DAY OF CHRIST JESUS (PHILIPPIANS 1:6, NASB).

What is the climate of your heart?
How do you place your confidence in God and continue to bear good fruit?

Pruning

Pruning is not my favorite garden chore. I feel a little cruel chopping off branches that the rose bushes have produced inch by inch and leaf by leaf. When we're through snipping, they look as though they've had a pretty severe haircut! Sooner or later, though, anything that is *not* pruned looks uncared for and unruly—and not very productive.

It was a certain apple tree I saw while walking through an orchard that illustrates to me that your pruning in my life is something not to be tolerated but to actually be desired. For as a tree, this apple tree had been diligently pruned and was quite small. Yet its branches were loaded with apples. It was a rack for fruit! It had more fruit than many larger trees with lofty branches. The smaller the tree (and the more pruned), the greater the fruit and harvest!

I see it as a picture of my life. Without your pruning, Lord, there is more of me and less of the fruit. With your pruning, there is less of me and more of the fruit! It's just that simple!

Attitudes, habits, my schedule? Unproductive time? Here I am, Lord; I'm volunteering for pruning. Snip away at anything that is hindering my growth. Trim away to make room for loads of the fruit of the Spirit. What a relief it is to be relieved of the burden of trying to become an impressive tree! Just keep pruning me until people who look at me see a rack for fruit!

"I AM THE TRUE GRAPEVINE, AND MY FATHER IS THE GARDENER. HE CUTS OFF EVERY BRANCH OF MINE THAT DOESN'T PRODUCE FRUIT, AND HE PRUNES THE BRANCHES THAT DO BEAR FRUIT SO THEY WILL PRODUCE EVEN MORE" (JOHN 15:1-2, NLT).

What can you trim away in your life to make room
for the abundant fruit of the Spirit?

_____

_____

_____

_____

_____

_____

_____

_____

_____

_____

_____

_____

_____

_____

_____

_____

_____

_____

The Blessings of Winter

Each season comes to my garden. Each with its beauty. Each with its promise for the next season. Seasons are never missed in the world of nature, but sometimes my life has weird weather. It seems that winter goes on year after year—broken only by a few days of balmy weather. It's hard to understand why it is winter in my life when I'm surrounded by everyone else's summer.

In the midst of my winter—where hope seems dormant and the resources of my heart seem dried up—I long for the brightness and safety of the past. I fret about the trying circumstances of the present and fear that the future may be colder and darker. The roots of my heart dig deeper into your Word, reaching for your heart, Lord. It is there that I tap into your life. Hope begins to course through the branches of my heart.

I am beginning to see that while my winter may not be a time of joyful planting or satisfying harvest, this season for putting down deeper and deeper roots of trust in you must not be wasted. Although it looks like the hope in my garden is sleeping, while I wait you are taking advantage of what has happened to me for my good. In the garden of my life, whether it is a carefree summer or a bleak winter that seems endless, hope is here because you are here surrounding me with the evidence of your love, faithfulness, and goodness. Yes, hope is here for me to gather, no matter the season.

In this process, my winters are becoming my treasures. They are the means by which I know you better. Winter is my season of growth. I am finding a new dimension of your character and fresh awareness of your love for me. "Thank you" is replacing "Why me?"

LET YOUR ROOTS GROW DOWN INTO HIM, AND LET YOUR LIVES BE BUILT ON HIM.
THEN YOUR FAITH WILL GROW STRONG IN THE TRUTH YOU WERE TAUGHT,
AND YOU WILL OVERFLOW WITH THANKFULNESS (COLOSSIANS 2:7, NLT).

What blessings come out of the process of winter seasons in your life?
Can you feel the warmth of hope as you trust in God's goodness and care?

_____

_____

_____

_____

_____

_____

_____

_____

_____

_____

_____

_____

_____

_____

_____

_____

_____

About the Author

Sandy Lynam Clough is both an author and an artist. She has written or illustrated twenty-eight gift books, selling over one million of them. A fourth generation artist, Sandy got her earliest art training and encouragement from her father and mother. She began selling her paintings as an art major at Mississippi College. Although she has a degree in art and a master's degree in art education, her heart was in painting instead of teaching. Mississippi College has twice named her Art Alumnus of the Year.

Sandy Clough creates beautifully realistic paintings and designs that are both fresh and contemporary, yet her painting is fine art. This combination of fresh and traditional is uniquely Sandy Clough and appears on many licensed products sold throughout the United States and also internationally. Both her art and her writing are inspired and grounded by her Christian faith. To learn more about Sandy Clough, visit her website at www.sandyclough.com.